Charles Eugene McKee

The new rapid

A light-line: Connective-vowel system of shorthand

Charles Eugene McKee

The new rapid
A light-line: Connective-vowel system of shorthand

ISBN/EAN: 9783337270117

Printed in Europe, USA, Canada, Australia, Japan

Cover: Foto ©Andreas Hilbeck / pixelio.de

More available books at **www.hansebooks.com**

THE
NEW + RAPID.

A LIGHT-LINE CONNECTIVE-VOWEL SYSTEM OF SHORTHAND
WRITTEN FROM PRINCIPLES WITHOUT THE USE
OF WORD SIGNS OR CONTRACTIONS

—— FOR ——

Commercial, Political and Judicial
RECORDING,

AND IN ALL THOSE FIELDS OF LABOR WHICH DEMAND THE
HIGHEST DEGREE OF SPEED AND LEGIBILITY.

BY C. E. McKEE,

Principal Short-Hand Department of the
COLLEGE OF COMMERCE, BUFFALO, N. Y.

PUBLISHED BY THE
BUFFALO PUBLISHING CO.
1888.

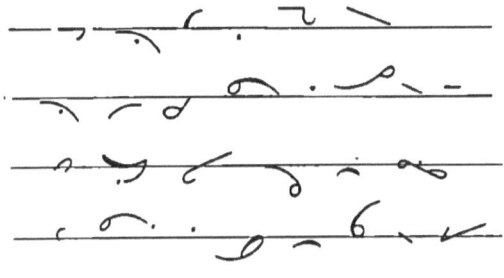

TRANSCRIPT.

Mighty thou art, O magic pen,
Thou who dost serve the wants of men;
By rescuing golden thoughts from spoil,
And saving the world from years of toil.

THE AUTHOR.

Preface.

No apology need be offered for the appearance of the present work. The history of the past proves that a system of brief writing has been the demand of the ages. That that demand still exists is too obvious to even need assertion. When we realize what a small per cent. of the multitudes who yearly take up the study of short-hand, make a success of it, we begin to see and realize the need of improvement in this line of human achievement. This recognized necessity for a simple, practical system of brief writing,—one that can be learned and put into daily use, by the masses, without devoting years of study and practice to this one branch alone—is what inspired the author in his efforts to develop the present system.

Says an eminent writer of recent date, "The formation of a really good system of short-hand has yet to be shown to the world." Whether the New Rapid fills this want or not is not for the author to say. Of one thing, however, he feels assured,—that the final success of any system depends upon true worth and merit. No amount of advertising, or high sounding statements, will render a worthless thing of practical value. And since experience has taught us that the best argument that can be put forth in favor of the New Rapid, is a knowledge of its merits, we feel that we have in some degree at least been successful in our efforts to found it upon true and lasting principles. It is to be hoped that it will not fall short of its object, namely: *To secure a shorter road to Stenographic success; to obtain greater legibility and speed, and lighten the labors of that mighty army that is daily growing in the skillful use of the pen.*

A glance will be sufficient, to enable one to see that the system is entirely different from those of the past, and that in it short-hand has been emancipated from the superstitions that have surrounded it from its birth to the present day.

For the purpose of giving the reader some knowledge of the principles of this system, and its many superior advantages, we give a brief review of it in the introduction. In referring the reader to this we ask that it be read with a fair, impartial, and unbiased spirit.

We think, aside from the principles of the system, there is much to commend the New Rapid, to those desiring to pursue the study of short-hand. The matter presented throughout the work has been carefully selected and graded. Unlike other systems, we have presented it in the form of Lessons. This arrangement will be of great assistance to the student. Whether it is pursued under an instructor or by home study, it enables the learner to take it up in its proper order. Each lesson is thoroughly mastered before going to the next, and as it contains a complete explanation of the subject in question, the student avoids the confusion arising from disconnected lessons. Everything belonging to a lesson is placed directly in connection with it, that the student may get the benefit of it just when it is needed. A list of questions is added after each lesson, which enables the student to ascertain if everything passed over has been thoroughly mastered. They also serve as good test questions when a hasty review on theory is desired.

Realizing that *practice* is what is necessary to render short-hand useful, we have presented a carefully selected list of words after each lesson. This enables the learner to get practice on those words that will tend to fix the principles of the lessons at hand, thoroughly in mind. The lists are so practical and comprehensive, that by the time the theory of the subject has been completed, the student will have acquired a large vocabulary of practical word forms.

Realizing what a vast number of the young men and women who pursue the study of short-hand, have not the opportunity to secure the services of an instructor, we have aimed to make the book a teacher of itself. We hope that all those who pursue the study will find in it truth and beauty, and a lasting degree of satisfaction in its practice.

With these few words of greeting, the system is commended to those whose labors it seeks to lessen, trusting that it may prove a faithful friend and servant, in all the fields of labor to which it may be called to administer.

Buffalo, N. Y., Dec. 13, 1888.

Introduction,

in which are set forth a few of the merits of The New Rapid, showing that the principles upon which it is founded are those that should govern a practical system of short-hand.

The burning desire of the human mind for increased knowledge, and consequently for improvement, seems to be the progressive principle, propelling us onward and upward. Improvements follow improvements on all the inventions of the times. Perfection in the arts, the sciences and the numberless inventions of the age, is the one grand idea that fills the mind of the scientific world.

The impossibilities of yesterday are probabilities to-day and possibilities to-morrow. The world is indeed moving onward and upward. But in her onward march, she has not forgotten the pen,—who, though "mightier than the sword,"—with our present long-hand method of recording thought, needs facilities to aid in coping with the modern methods of living. In modern short-hand—The New Rapid—she has found this aid, which presents to the world an alphabet of letters so simple and facile, that even a child may learn to write. This method of writing is as wonderful as it is simple. By it, speech is recorded as it falls from the lips of the rapid speaker, and thus the finest sentiments of the human soul,—as the poet says,—

> "Are transmitted to glowing pages,
> And handed down to future ages."

What once meant to the literary man years of laborious toil, is now a pleasant task, requiring but a few weeks time for its completion. The man of business who formerly toiled all day at his desk, can to-day dispatch his correspondence in an hour's time. And instead of it being a miserable scrawl, impossible to decipher, it appears in a neat type, as plain and legible as a printed book.

A spark of truth, now kindled into a blaze, shoots forth its rays from an elevated light house, casting brilliant streams of light over a clouded stenographic world. As the effusion of spreading light breaks in upon the darkness, gilding the once blackened clouds of doubt and failure, from the advancing host "ring out in peals of accent loud and clear," Eureka! Eureka!

Although the art of short-hand has done much in the past, yet its history shows that to those who have followed it, it has been very unsatisfactory. Years of study and practice, directed towards this one branch alone, was the only way it could be made available; and even then without persistent practice, it was all forgotten in less than one-tenth of the time it took to acquire it. The large percentage of those who have made a total failure of shorthand, even after earnest and determined effort, is sufficient to show that something better is wanted in this direction. The fact that even those who *do* master it thoroughly, seldom have confidence enough in its legibility to use it in recording thoughts for safe keeping, is enough to show why it has never come into practical everyday use.

What the world is demanding to-day is a system that can be *easily learned*, is as *legible as print*, and can be *written rapidly*. Illegibility has been the most glaring defect of all systems of short-hand writing. This great deficiency, together with others, so painfully realized by the author in past years, accounts for the existence of the New Rapid shorthand. In this we are fully justified in saying that a great improvement has been made and that short-hand is now placed upon a firmer and more practical basis than ever before.

Since the New Rapid system is so much unlike others, we review briefly a few of its prominent features,—that the reader may become acquainted with the underlying principles and better understand why a new system of short-hand has been born, and is working such a mighty revolution throughout the civilized world.

At the outset, we wish to say that if you are a writer of some other system, we hope you will lay aside all prejudices and predilections, and judge candidly of the merits of the New Rapid. We say this, knowing how apt Stenographers are to consider the system they write, as the *ne plus ultra* of perfection, and bar out all facts that would tend to make it appear otherwise. All that is claimed for the New Rapid, can be fully and satisfactorily demonstrated; and hence we ask that you reason candidly with yourself, while we explain briefly a few of its merits.

The present system is the result of much study and research, coupled with the sincere belief that there are important springs of truth yet unexplored, connected with the science of swift writing. The system has been perfected and brought to its high state of excellence, only through the firmly established principles, that govern so harmoniously all its parts.

Over one year was spent in constructing and arranging the Phonographic Alphabet. To the inexperienced this may seem like an exorbitant waste of time and energy; but there are many difficulties to be encountered in developing a system of writing that will record briefly and systematically,—and in such an easy, simple manner,—human speech as rapidly as it is spoken.

The success of anything depends largely upon the foundation. Nowhere is this truer than in short-hand; and as the alphabet is the foundation of the whole structure, it is necessary that it contain those elements that will conduce largely toward bringing the system as a whole into a high state of perfection. Realizing this, we have spared no pains to lay a foundation that will be simple, practical and complete. The philosophical arrangement of our alphabet, combined with the powerful contracting principles, is what enables us to secure such a remarkable degree of brevity without sacrificing legibility.

J. M. Sloan, of England, author of Sloan-Duployan Short-hand, has truthfully said: "It does not require great intelligence to understand that the more powerful an alphabet is, the fewer abbreviations are required; consequently more sounds are retained, which give extra legibility." Since the alphabet forms the foundation and is of such vital importance to all the after-work, we here illustrate a few of its prominent features.

One of the main characteristics of this system is the easy, running style of writing produced, and the great similarity it bears to long-hand. A writer of prominence has said: "The greatest perfection of long-hand consists in its free, easy style, and regularity of appearance." This is a recognized fact; and since the hand is accustomed to the long-hand style of writing, it is obvious that the nearer short-hand approaches this, the easier and more natural will it be in execution. Recognizing this as one of the essentials requisite to easy rapid writing, this system has been based upon the principles governing long-hand. Curves, instead of being parts of circles, are, as in long-hand, elliptical; and the writing as a whole tends toward the right, producing an easy running style.

INTRODUCTION.

This similarity to long-hand is still further carried out by discarding the use of shaded characters. Too many shaded strokes renders the writing very difficult of execution. If in long-hand we should attempt to shade every downward stroke, which would be every other stroke, we would find it a very slow and laborious way of writing. Hence, the fewer shaded strokes employed the better. In view of this fact we have constructed an alphabet which practically does away with shading. This we consider in many ways a great improvement over former systems. In the *Pitmanic systems, every other letter is a shaded stroke. This of course necessitates a great amount of shading, which is antagonistic to easy rapid execution.

But by other means equally important, we have succeeded in securing to a still larger degree that ease and grace in execution which so characterizes the long-hand style of writing. This is accomplished by the manner in which certain letters are represented.

In assigning values to the different strokes, the easiest and most facile outlines were selected to represent the most frequently recurring sounds. Thus s and z, which are found most frequently in the English language, are represented by horizontal strokes ; and t and d, which rank second, by right oblique strokes running the same as the strokes in long-hand, which can be struck either upwards or downwards. And so on throughout the alphabet — easy, facile strokes are utilized in representing frequently recurring sounds. This enables us, not only to write common phraseology with exceeding ease

---

* By Pitmanic syetems is meant those systems which use the alphabet of consonants as arranged by Isaac Pitman, of England, in 1837. They are the Graham's, Munson's, Scott Browne's, Ben Pitman's, Burn's, etc.

and facility, but it secures *lineality*, one of the great essentials to easy rapid writing.

In all the Pitmanic systems the most frequently recurring sounds in the language are, unfortunately, represented by the most difficult characters. For example, the s and z, and t and d, are expressed by perpendicular strokes, while other letters are represented by values wholly unsuited for easy joining and so impracticable that they necessitate the use of special hooks. Throughout the entire alphabet, practicability is wholly ignored.

A perpendicular stroke, and especially a curved one,— such as represents the s and z in the Pitmanic systems—is the most difficult line it is possible to form. The hand in its right and left eliptical movements naturally conforms to the law of movement in long-hand, and rebels against all efforts to form a perpendicular stroke. In view of these facts we have virtually discarded the use of perpendicular lines. This disuse of long perpendicular strokes and the values assigned to those easy in execution, is what renders the movements in the writing of the New Rapid, so much like that employed in long-hand. The result is that it can be written easily and rapidly, with but little practice as compared with those systems which employ so many complex outlines written in an upright manner.

The disadvantages arising from the use of perpendicular strokes and especially to represent sounds of such frequent recurrence, are more fully realized when we know what long, irregular and difficult outlines are produced in writing.

To illustrate this point we give a line of words in which perpendicular strokes occur as written in the Pitmanic systems. The first line is the Pitmanic writing and the second that of the New Rapid. Observe not only the absence of perpen-

INTRODUCTION. 15

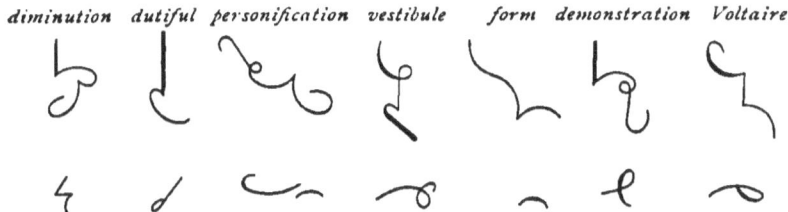

dicular strokes in the writing of the New Rapid, but also the great degree in which brevity and lineality is secured. It is also proper to remark that the writing of the New Rapid is much more legible than that of the Pitmanic.

Next we desire to make mention of the simple and practical manner in which all words are written. They are not, as in other systems, committed as word forms and contractions, but are written from principle as in long-hand. It might appear to a casual observer, that in this way, a degree of brevity equal to other systems would not be secured. But the fact is there is not a system in existence that can cope with the New Rapid in securing brevity, and yet so successfully retain the legibility.

By this simple, practical manner of writing, the reporter is enabled to write any word, by applying the underlying principles, and is not as in other systems, compelled to resort to a phonographic dictionary, for the writing of every new word that comes up. It would be just as reasonable for a student to attempt to commit the solution and answer of the numberless problems in mathematics, when by understanding a few underlying principles, he could solve any problem that might be proposed.

That word-signs and arbitrary contractions, are detrimental to a system of short-hand, needs no argument to prove. The writers of all systems realize this. Late works on the Pitmanic systems show that authors are trying to lessen these signs in number. But the result of their efforts, in this direction is very unsatisfactory. The fundamental principles of the Pitmanic systems are such that it is impossible to secure sufficient brevity by writing from principle. Hence the use of word-signs and contractions, in these systems, is by no means a choice, but a necessity. It is obvious, too, that by the new method a great amount of time and labor is saved. The most arduous task found in connection with the study of short-hand has been the memorizing of the countless number of word-signs and contractions. This old method of memorizing word-signs and contractions by the hundreds has been found too slow and laborious, and has consequently given way to the more modern and practical method, viz.: that of *writing from principle*, instead of arbitrary signs. The fulness of the writing and the close resemblance that the movement bears to long-hand is the crowning feature of the New Rapid.

The next subject in order of importance, is, that this is a connective vowel system. That is, vowels are expressed by strokes the same as consonants, and words are written without lifting the pen. This is one of the distinguishing features of this system,—one which promotes facility in writing and legibility in reading. In the Pitmanic systems, vowels are expressed by dots and dashes placed in a certain position after the consonants are written, but in order to obtain speed sufficient for even moderate writing, the writer finds it impossible to go back after writing every word, and add one, two and sometimes three dots or dashes of a certain size, and in a certain position. Hence the vowels must be omitted, and are used only on an average of about once in seventy-five words. The result is, the writer is not only left to read his notes without vowels, which are as essential to legibility as consonants, but is compelled to go through the long and arduous task of learning what is known in those systems as "vocalization" and "revocalization," all of which must be practically abandoned when he enters the field of actual practice. The expediency of connective vowel strokes is apparent to everybody. The writing of words in a broken and disconnected manner is wholly unphilosophical.

In matter of speed acquired by connective strokes we quote the language of an eminent writer, on the disadvantages of pen-lifting: "The act of pen-lifting is quite complex. In addition to lifting the pen, moving it along a little space, and re-applying it to the paper, there are the mental acts of ending one word and beginning another. Of course all these processes may be executed quickly; but time is time, it is not easy to estimate a point like this; but probably a pen-lifting requires as much time as the writing of two strokes, possibly three. One pen-lifting, it is true, even estimated as above, does not require much time; but many hundreds or thousands occurring in close succession are a very serious draw-back. Hence anything that reduces the number of pen-liftings is very favorable to high speed." We take great pleasure in quoting the above lines, as they are from the pen of one of the most able Pitmatic writers in this country. They were written referring particularly to phrase-writing, showing the advantages to be gained in a system of short-hand by connecting words. These words do not lack in weight and meaning. If it is advantageous to combine different words, how much more so is it, to write simple words themselves without lifting the pen. Had these words even been directed in particular at the Pitmanic manner of writing vowels, they could not have struck a more severe blow at the very foundation of these systems. The sterling truth of such words are recognized by all experienced writers. But for a writer of these systems to admit them, is to strike a blow at the most glaring defect in Phonography.

In matter of legibility, we quote from the English writer, J. M. Sloan. He says: "I maintain that no system can be legible that does not either insert or indicate the vowel in its exact position in every word." These words do not need commenting upon. Their truth is self-evident.

This question of illegibility, and loss of speed resulting from disconnected vowels brings us to the subject of Vowel Position, which in this system differs very radically from the Pitmanic. The complex and uncertain manner of using position in these systems of Phonography has led some to ask if they were not really of more hindrance than assistance. And reasonably may they make such inquiries; for each position is assigned four or five different sounds, which are taken from as many different vowels. For example, a consonant stroke written on what is called the first position might express broad a, long e, short i, short o, long i, or oi. In reading, the context must determine which of these vowels is to be used, and also the place it occupies in the word; for in most cases there is nothing to show whether the words begin with a vowel or consonant, or where the vowel is located. The result of such indefinite and uncertain writing is that a half dozen different words are frequently expressed by the same outline. In this particular point the Pitmanic systems could not possibly be more deficient. What few vowels that are even expressed by positions are so indefinite that they are about as bad as none at all. In the New Rapid system no room for such confusion is allowed. Each position is assigned but one vowel, and the place that vowel occupies in the word is an absolute certainty. And further, instead of the vowel positions being a scale of conglomerate sounds, they are arranged in their natural alphabetical order. This method of position is so simple that students learn, and are able to use it, with but a few minutes study. But what is equally perplexing to the students of the Graham, Pitman, and other systems is, that they are not taught the subject of position until they have become perfectly familiar with all the principles. Then just as the learner is beginning to write easily, and has a settled form of writing, he is ushered into the mysterious realm of position, where invisible a, e, i, o, i, and oi, are all placed on one position. Here he is compelled to unlearn a great deal of what has already been acquired, by writing words differently and on position. The same can be said of word-signs and contractions. There being such a large number of these, they are left until the learner has mastered most of the principles of the system. Here he learns one way to write these words, but in order to gain sufficient speed, he must now commit brief signs for the representation of hundreds of words and thousands of contractions.

Any system of instruction, which teaches in one lesson that which must necessarily be abandoned in the next, is certainly far from being founded upon rational principles. In the New Rapid the student learns things in the beginning just as they will be, when carried into practice. Not a single word form is taught, in any part of the work that will be changed later on. It is surprising how indelibly forms first committed are stamped upon the memory; and to attempt to forget the old, and learn a new, must end in utter confusion. It is at this point that so many have in the past dropped the study of short-hand, dissatisfied and discouraged with its multitudinous perplexities. The elimination of this fault so common to other systems is a principle of which the New Rapid can justly feel proud.

Another fact well worth mentioning, wherein this system differs from others, is that the q, and x, have each a character of their own. The Pitmanic systems have no x or q but use ks for x and kw for q. This manner of writing these letters requires two strokes to express, what is represented in English by one letter. Besides the inconvenience in writing and reading, they are the most difficult combinations to analyze phonetically that the student meets with in all his study. Who is there who does not find it difficult at first to perceive that in x there are the sounds of k and s, or in q the sounds k and w? Since these sounds are so closely united and represented in English by one letter, it is found much easier both in reading and writing short-hand, to have them represented by one simple stroke. But the most perplexing part of all of it is that in reading, one could not tell whether the ks stood for x, kis kes, oks oaks, aks kas, or any other similar combination. And further, when it comes to the matter of saving time in writing (which is the sole aim of short-hand), the manner in which they are written is of no small consequence. To illustrate this in point of brevity, we give below a few words as written in other systems. The first line is the Pitmanic manner of writing these words, and the second line that of the New Rapid.

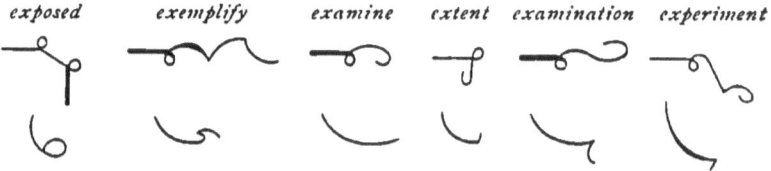

exposed   exemplify   examine   extent   examination   experiment

The writing of these words in this system is not only briefer, but much more legible than the Pitmanic, since they contain all the sounds in the words. And these words are by no means exceptions. The letters q and x should not be separated into their elements, and written thus, any more than the diphthongs or double consonants.

And even further, to say nothing of the gain in legibility and brevity, words in this system are represented by much more facile outlines than in others. Such difficult, irregular outlines as are seen in some of the words given above can not be found in the whole realm of the New Rapid short-hand writing. It will thus be seen that there is everything in favor of expressing the q and x as they are in this system, while by the old method not a single point is gained.

Another important and distinctive feature of this system is the remarkable degree in which analogy is preserved in the writing of primitive and derivative words. This is a subject of vital importance to the short-hand writer and which has unfortunately been overlooked by former authors. For example, when we learn how to write the word *educate*, it is obvious that upon rational principles all derivatives, such as *educated*, *education*, *educational*, should be written in a similar manner, at least as far as the sounds are alike.

In some systems the derivatives of such words are so entirely changed in outline from the primitive that no similarity whatever is traceable. This necessitates learning forms wholly unlike one another for the purpose of expressing words closely allied not only in sound, but also in meaning. This method sets all law at defiance and results in utter confusion, both in writing and reading. But there is another class of derivatives known as negatives, in distinction from positive, the writing of which is even more important, since there is such a great difference in meaning, yet such a similarity in sound. In this class of words the positive is the primitive and the negative word the derivative. For example, the words *legal, moral,* and *content* are positive, while *illegal, immoral,* and *discontent* are the negatives. Of this class of words there is a very large number in practical use; and since the main parts of the words are alike in sound, yet just the opposite in meaning, it is necessary in observing the laws of analogy, to have their outline, in the main, similar; and yet, for the sake of legibility, a difference should be unmistakably expressed. In this system all these requirements are met, and the result is that the most difficult words the stenographer meets with in other systems, are, in this, written by one simple rule, which can be told in less than a dozen words. They are also written with a brevity and legibility unparalleled.

But perhaps the reader is not aware of the immense amount of labor and practice that is saved by our method of writing these words. A large per cent. of the English language is composed of derivative words. In other systems, where these are written at variance to all law, and their difference expressed arbitrarily, it is necessary to learn each and every word or sign separately. When written as in this system, which is wholly unlike all others in this respect, the writer learns only the primitive or positive word, and the writing of the derivative or negative is as easy and natural as is the defining of derivative words when we know the primitive. Thus all that is necessary, is to be able to write the primitive. The derivative, which is but a slight modification of the same word, can be written without previous practice and on the spur of the moment. This saves the stenographer the learning of hundreds of word-forms, and writes them easily and legibly in accordance with the fundamental law of the system—*from principle.*

Another point well worth mentioning, is the manner in which all coalescents are written. In the English language there are nearly thirty double consonants, occurring as *pr* in *pray*, *bl* in *blame*, *sp* in *spy*, etc. The writing of these in most systems is very complex and uncertain, as the learner is compelled to commit new forms for the representation of many of these coalescents. To conform to rule and be in any way consistent, with the writing of the separate letters of which they are composed, they should be expressed by some simple modification of one or more of these letters rather than by new characters bearing no relation whatever. This system fully accomplishes this and writes all coalescents in accordance with the laws of analogy, and from principles which can be explained, and comprehended by a mere beginner in a few minutes time.

Thus it will be observed that the intricately, and judicially constructed alphabet, is the foundation to the whole structure. No new and complex characters are introduced at different stages of the work, but instead, the system is built up scientifically from a phonographic alphabet. We believe this to be the true foundation, upon which all systems should be developed. It is reasonable, it is practical, it is in keeping with the development of other sciences.

Another merit common only to this system is the fact that every letter or sound has a distinct and separate character of its own. Each character is allowed to stand for but one sound, and is never used for any other. In the Pitmanic systems a hook has seven different values. That is, a hook turned at the beginning of a stroke adds an r. Turned on the opposite side it adds an l. A similar hook written after certain strokes represents n. Written after still another class of letters it stands for the ending *tive*. After still another class of letters it represents f or v. Turned on other particular letters a trifle larger and it expresses w, and the same hook after any stroke expresses the common termination *shun*. No wonder the common saying among Stenographers to beginners was: "If you don't get stuck on the hooks you are all right." It does not require much intelligence to see that such a multitude of different values assigned to the same character, even though changed a trifle in shape or size, would end in utter confusion. This is one of the most common defects of short-hand systems. Even those, which aim to write more from principles—Porter's, Eclectic, Pernin, Bishop's and Sloan-DuPloyan—fall into the same error. They not only allow the same characters to represent different sounds, but introduce at various stages new characters, almost, if not altogether, identical with those already given which are allowed to represent different letters or combinations of letters. Especially is this true of what is known as the Eclectic system. Characters already utilized in the representation of sounds are used for whole syllables which have no relation or dependence whatever upon the original value assigned. The Eclectic and Sloan-DuPloyan abound with these arbitary and deficient methods of securing brevity.

The Eclectic system claims to write from principle, but when all that is really arbitrary is stricken from it, there is little left of what can be called principle. It is without doubt one of the most illegible systems in existence. Every sound in the language is assigned a position and the result is, to conform to the fundamental principles, every word in the language must be written on a particular position. Since it has been found impossible to secure speed, from the use of so much position, phrasing has been introduced, which necessarily abandons the use of position in so far as it is employed, and defeats the very purpose of the fundamental principle of the system. It has one merit, however, for which it should receive credit, and that is, the running style of writing that is produced.

The utter illegibility of short-hand systems of the past, without some clue to the subject matter, is what has rendered short-hand of so little value in practical everyday use. The motto of the New Rapid from the beginning to the end is, *legibility*.

As further conducing toward perfect legibility is the fact that in this system the writing runs to the right, producing perfect lineality, and can be written on the different positions without occupying more than one-half of the space perpendicularily that it does in the Pitmanic systems. Experienced writers will see at a moment's glance, what great advantages are derived from this easy continuous style of writing. A lack of this in other systems is, as all know, the most serious drawback in gaining speed, and the very reason why phrasing — *a go-as-you-please style* — must be resorted to.

Since the word Phonography means writing by sound, it is generally supposed that these systems styled Phonographic systems, more properly called, however, Pitmanic systems, write phononetically. But it is as far from being the case as day is from night. True, they have material by which words may be written out phonetically, but when put to practical use, this is found wholly impossible. Not one word in a hundred is written phonetically. The very foundation of the systems will not permit it. Their disconnected vowels, with complex and indefinite positions, together with sound value unsuited for contractions of frequent recurrence, make the subject of phonetic writing, owing to a lack of brevity, wholly impossible. We mention this to show that although this system is not called Phonography, it comes nearer the meaning of the term, practically, than any of these so-called systems.

This is perhaps more forcibly realized when we remember that in many cases one outline is used for a half dozen different words. In some of these systems words as far apart in sound and meaning, as *had, dollar, do, defendant* and *did*, are all written with the same outline. In the Pitmanic systems the following twenty-nine words: *creature, occurred, court, cared, accurate, curried, cured, cord, chord, accord, according, crate, crowd, acrid, crout, card, cart, carried, accrued, occured, curt, curd, euchred, coward, cried, caret, accrete, crowed* and *crude*, are all written with the same outline; while those systems called practical Phonographic systems, which omit the shade, would add the following eighteen words to the above list: *gored, gourd, great, grate, grade, girt, gird, grout, groat, greet, greed, agreed, augured, grot, geared, garret, grit* and *guard.* This would make a total of forty-seven different words, all of which are written from the same outline. And what is still more absurd is the fact that many of these words have no similarity of sound whatever, and yet they are written by systems called *Phonographic systems.* These illustrations show how utterly Phonography fails, practically in being consistent with the name its writers so highly worship, and so earnestly covet.

In the face of all these glaring deficiencies is it any wonder that such statements as the following emanate from the very writers of these impracticable systems: "In so far as American short-hand is built upon the Pitmanic foundation, I wish to point out that it is necessarily mixed up with the most absurdly unpracticable notions with which an essentially practical art was ever encumbered."

That the truth of our statements as to the relative merits of the New Rapid may be more apparent, we give illustrations of short-hand writing by the standard Pitmanic systems of to-day, The following sentence is taken from Graham's text-book as written by himself in the briefest reporting style which that system affords:

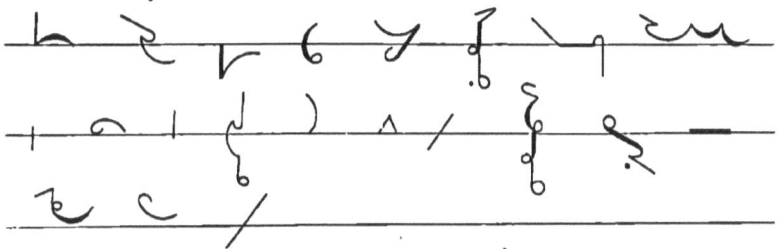

The writing of the above sentence is quite brief, but as to legibility it is perfectly ridiculous. It would be impossible to read it even if written out in long-hand. That the reader may see why this is so, we give the sentence in print as spelled and phrased above in short-hand. It is as follows: *tmp pnf dl ths njshun* **onthe** *dstrsing pktr* **of***wnndvd bt mlt t tnthts s ou ch* **ofall***thsdstrs sbnhpt g* **ona***sng fld.*

The person who can make out a half dozen of the above words is certainly entitled to a high rank in the clairvoyant field. It is impossible even to get any idea of what is intended to be expressed. Those few short words printed in heavy face type are the only ones that can be read and they are represented by special characters, and hence in so far as being founded upon the alphabet and written from principles they represent nothing at all.

The New Rapid writes the above sentence out in full as follows:

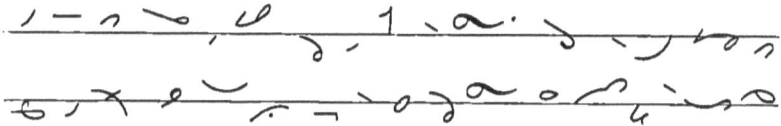

The above writing represents all the principle sounds in the sentence. That this may be contrasted with the Graham writing, we give the sentence in print as written in the New Rapid. It is as follows: *It ma be panfl to dwel thus in imagnshn onthe distresing pikr of wun individl but multply it tenthousand tims sa how much of all this distres hasbeen hept togthr ona singl feld.*

The writing of this sentence in this system is not only briefer and more legible than the Graham but in all those essentials requisite to rapid writing it stands first.

Although the gain in brevity is great, yet this is small in comparison with other existing qualities in favor of the New Rapid. As written in the Graham's it contains nineteen angles, while as written in the New Rapid it contains but six. Graham's writing contains thirteen full shaded strokes, while the New Rapid employs but three minor shades. The Graham writing contains sixteen perpendicular outlines, the New Rapid contains but one. The Graham writing contains fifteen word-signs, the New Rapid two. The Graham writing is contracted, phrased, and jumbled together until it is wholly illegible reading from principle. The New Rapid is written out containing nearly every sound in the sentence. All of these fundamental requisites to successful and easy writing are illustrated and their merits shown to be phenominally in favor of the New Rapid in a sentence of but thirty-seven words.

Following is a sentence taken from Munson's text-book, page 187, which is reproduced exactly as written by the author.

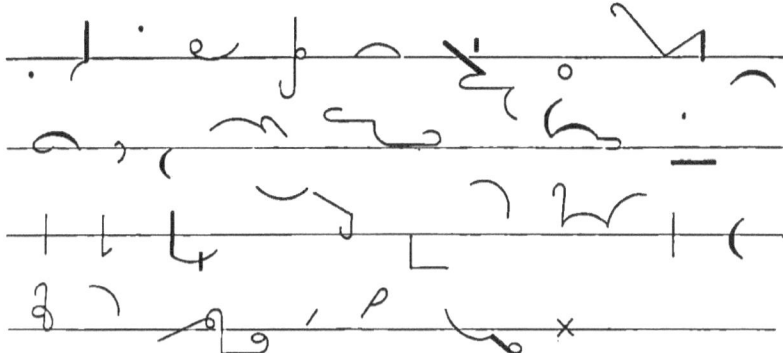

This sentence is written out in full in the New Rapid as follows:

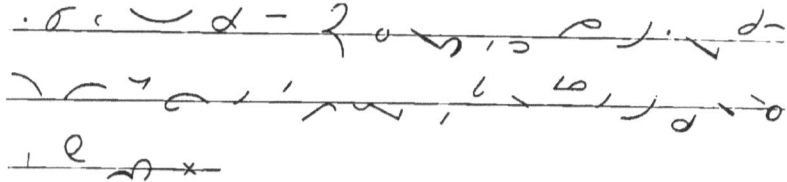

The above is translated as follows: *The adult and sane testator may bequeath his property to whom he will, with the important qualification that he can not give it to a donee incompetent to take or trammel it with trusts or restrictions which the statute forbids.*

Munson's writing of this sentence contains seventy-five characters, while in the New Rapid it is written in full with but fifty-seven characters.

In this one sentence Munson employs eighteen perpendicular strokes. The New Rapid employs but one, and that a minute tick.

The great gain in this system over others is more striking when we realize what they would amount to in the course of a sermon or lecture.

In taking down an address of less than forty minutes length, there would be a gain in the New Rapid of at least fifteen-hundred characters.

There would be at least eighteen-hundred angles less than in others. The New Rapid would gain over two-thousand perpendicular strokes, fourteen-hundred shaded strokes and eighteen-hundred word-signs, to say nothing of the great gain in legibility.

Before leaving this subject we desire to illustrate one more point. As compared with other systems the New Rapid makes very little use of phrasing. The writing in this system is more capable of successful phrasing than in the majority of others, but since its use is so detrimental to legibility, and since even without it this system is capable of a higher rate of speed than others, the New Rapid takes pride in being able to avoid this dangerous ground.

The following phrases, taken from Pitman's Companion, illustrate how illegible writing becomes when phrased, and that even by its use other systems can not compete with the New Rapid in securing brevity. The first line is the Pitmanic writing and the second that of the New Rapid.

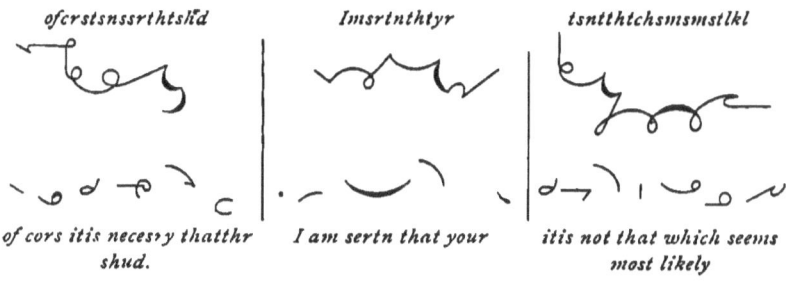

The italic letters above and below show the sounds represented by the writing in the respective systems.

It will be observed that the New Rapid writing is not only much more legible, but that it is also briefer in outline. The Pitman writing employs thirty-two strokes, the New Rapid twenty-seven. But even this is not all; phrasing is a study of itself which requires weeks of practice in order to make any practical use of it. In this system all this time is saved and in the end the writer has the assurance of knowing that he can read his notes.

We regret that time and space will not permit us to speak further in regard to the relative merits of the New Rapid. Though extended as our remarks may appear, they contain little in comparison with what could be easily said in favor of the principles embodied in the New Rapid. Not only have many points been omitted, but even those mentioned were quickly passed over, and but partially developed. The rest we leave for those who have the time and inclination to acquaint themselves more fully with its merits. That which has already been said, we hope, will inspire the learner to inquire further into its many hidden beauties, and induce him to master this study which is so useful in all the avocations of life.

We cannot close without quoting a few lines from D. S. Davies, of England, who has spent a quarter of a century in the study of the fundamental requisites to a system of shorthand. He says: "I have come to the conclusion, that the short-hand of the future will necessarily be based on the ordinary *roman long-hand;* that this beautiful writing contains *much greater* power than the geometric basis, which has been the basis of all English and American short-hand systems until very recently.

"All the necessary vowel sounds will be described in their natural order *without lifting* the pen. Present systems generally write the consonants first, and afterwards peg around them the vowels. This I think, is their *fundamental* error.

"Word-signs or grammalogues will be avoided.

"The short-hand alphabet must be *itself* short, so that there would not be much need of shortening afterwards."

These are sterling words from one who knows whereof he speaks. Similar prevailing opinions among the Stenographers of to-day could be given. But these are sufficient. They spring from a reliable source and run as parallel to the principles of the New Rapid as is possible for theory and practice to be united.

In our remarks we have been compelled through a sense of justice, to make comparisons with other systems. In doing so, however, we have aimed to show them in their true light. It has not been our wish or intention to underrate the value of former systems.

The invention of Phonography in 1837 marked a new era in Stenographic work. The great change it brought about in short-hand is admired by all. But, as Edward Pocknell has said, "We are not going to stop at Phonography." It will soon be like the sickle and spinning wheel, a thing of the past. We say this on good grounds, and with a firm belief in its truth. The signs of the times is pointing towards it. Nor is it a mere matter of chance, or the world's desire for something new; but on the contrary the change and drift of the times has a just and definable reason. *The foundation of the Pitmanic systems is wrong. This is becoming a recognized fact.*

The present system is not claimed to be the *ultima thule* to which improvement can be carried. But the points herein briefly mentioned *are* merits which we *do* claim, are, in the light of science, improvements in the right direction. They fall in line with the chain of improvements in other fields, that mark the progress of human achievement in this, the nineteenth century. No present system can show such simplicity in all its parts. It may be said of it as of nature, — *harmony reigns supreme.*

In the light of even these few briefly stated facts, may it not be said, and justly, that we have been remarkably successful in removing the recognized objectionable features of its predecessors, and placing it upon a firm and practical basis.

We are not of that number who, because of their own achievements, disregard the opinions of others.

On the contrary we rejoice to hear the notes of reform and improvement, and heartily contend for *truth* and *right.* We hope the time will soon come when in this art as well as in science and religion, we will march in the van of one mighty column, — keeping time with the music of the spheres, and guided as they, by the Author and Designer of Life.

Suggestions to the Student.

If the student has read the preceding introduction carefully, and obtained a clear idea of the fundamental principles governing the system, the following Lessons will be easy, and readily understood. Every hour given to practice and study, will come laden with a rich reward of satisfaction, as the student sees himself progressing from the slow and cumbersome style of long-hand, to the mastery of one so swift, useful, and beautiful.

It is very important that the student form correct habits at the beginning of his study and practice. He should attempt but one thing at a time, and master it completely. To make a practical use of short-hand it is necessary to practice every principle over and over until all words coming under it, can be written without the least hesitancy. More Stenographers fail to become proficient from a neglect of *practice*, than from any thing else.

The author has spared no pains to give everything in the following lessons that is necessary to a complete mastery of the system. Large and comprehensive lists of practical words have been introduced in connection with each lesson for the purpose of developing and securing familiarity with the principles. The mastery of the writing of these is the cornerstone to success, and the student should exercise the greatest pains to accomplish this end. The lists are so comlete that perfect familiarity with their writing will enable the student to write and read readily from a large vocabulary.

That practice makes perfect, is truer in short-hand than in any other branch of study. As in learning to write longhand, however, the practice must be directed to a definite and specific purpose. The shortest road to the mastery of shorthand is by *intelligent, persevering* practice.

SUGGESTIONS TO THE STUDENT.

The beginner should make haste slowly. That is, in practice, strive to make all strokes well, and not to leave a lesson until it is thoroughly mastered. A high rate of speed in writing comes as a result of familiarity gained by repeated practice. Not that a slow dragging movement should be used, but on the contrary every stroke should be formed from the beginning as quickly as is consistent with good form.

Do not become discouraged. Remember you are learning an entirely new system of writing, and you should not expect to learn it in a few short lessons. "Rome was not built in a day." Nor should you expect to reach the summit of stenographic success by one single effort.

Beginners are not apt to realize the importance of securing brief outlines for words, since short-hand, even in its elementary lessons, is so much briefer than long-hand. It should be remembered however that anything that will save pen-movements will enable the writer to write with a higher rate of speed, and by virtue of the brevity write better and more legibly. Hence, when words capable of being written more than one way, present themselves, they should be expressed in the shortest possible form consistent with legibility.

One of the chief advantages of the New Rapid is that all words are formed by definite rules, and hence they can be written and read successfully just in proportion to the thoroughness of which the governing principles are understood. Let your motto be, "One thing at a time and that well."

The student should cultivate the habit of inquiring into the why's and wherefore's of every principle. If this is done, and the object and purpose of everything thoroughly understood, the pupil holds the key which unlocks the hidden beauties in this unique and practical system of short-hand.

Principles.

First.—One of the fundamental principles of short-hand is a simplified alphabet. The characters which represent the different sounds are taken from straight and curved lines, which are written in three main directions.

ILLUSTRATIONS.

The curved strokes are, as in long-hand, parts of ellipses.

ILLUSTRATIONS.

There are three classes of letters, *long, short* and *surface characters.*

ILLUSTRATIONS.

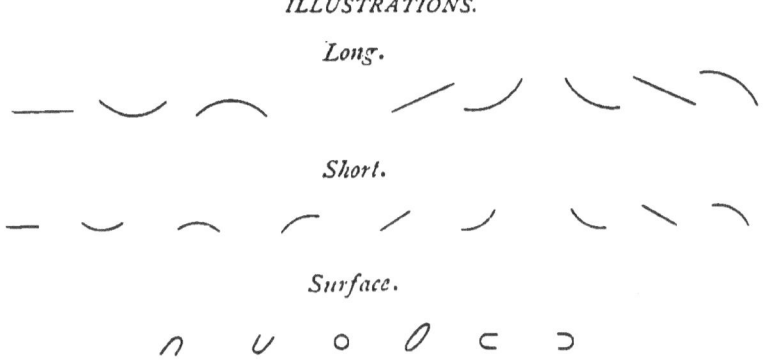

PHONOGRAPHIC ALPHABET.

Consonants.

P	B	T	D	Ch	J	K	G
pay	bay	tall	doll	choke	joke	cab	gab

F	V	S	Z	Th	Sh	Wh
fan	van	seal	zeal	the	rush	when

L	R	M	N	Ng	Q	X
lay	ray	moon	noon	ring	quill	excite

W	Y	H
way	yea	he

Vowels.

a	e	i	o	u
ă	ĕ	ĭ	ōō	ŭ

Diphthongs.

aw	oi	ou
saw	boy	now

PRACTICAL PHONOGRAPHIC ALPHABET.

Second.—Another principle, of no less importance, is Phonetic Spelling, i. e., spelling by sound. The English language contains about forty practical elementary sounds; and since words are written phonetically, it is necessary to have a character to represent each sound.

On the page to the right will be found the complete Phonographic Alphabet. This contains all the different characters that are used throughout the system, which are assigned to the sounds of the language in such a manner as to secure speed, legibility and simplicity in their highest degree.

It will be observed that the difference between *long* and *short* vowels is the slant and length. The long vowels are written upwards, and consequently a trifle longer and more slanting than the short vowels, which are written downwards. This is a result of the law of movement; and hence it should be borne in mind, that upward strokes are always longer and more slanting than the downward strokes.

It will be seen by the complete alphabet on the right hand page that *l* and *s* have each two different forms. This is for the purpose of facilitating the joining of letters and securing more powerful contractions, since these letters are so frequent in occurrence. The *c* and *s* are written alike, excepting a slight increase in the curvature of *c*. Hard *c* always has the sound of *k*. Soft *c* has the sound of *s*, as in since (sins); hence *c* proper is never used excepting when it stands alone as an initial letter in names or as an abbreviation.

COMPLETE PHONOGRAPHIC ALPHABET
CONTAINING ALL OF THE CHARACTERS.

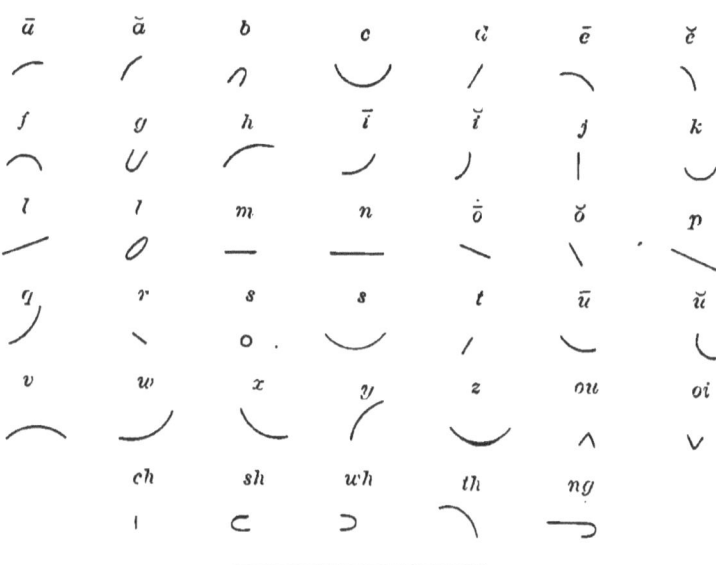

DIRECTION OF STROKES.

It is very important that the student learn at the outset the proper direction of writing each character. The *h* and *w* are written upwards while the *y* and *q* are drawn downwards.

The *a*, *i*, *t* and *d* are generally drawn downwards. All other characters are drawn to the right in the easiest possible manner.

These characters should be practiced over and over until the learner can write the entire alphabet correctly without referring to a copy at the rate of two alphabets per minute.

PEN-HOLDING.

The pen or pencil should be held in an easy, natural manner. The movement employed in this system is so similar to that of long-hand that the same position of the pen or pencil can be used with perfect freedom. It is not necessary, however, that the holder points over the right shoulder as in long-hand, but may be allowed to run on a line with the arm. This enables the writer to shade a stroke in any direction with an equal degree of facility. In writing with the pen, shading will be found easier if the face of the pen is rolled a trifle towards the body, or held between the first and second fingers, so that the letters *d* and *p* can be shaded at any point without changing the position, thus:

If the stenographic lead pencil is used, by the use of which an upward stroke can be shaded with almost the same facility as the downward, it matters little as to just how the pencil is held so long as the main position of the body, hand and paper is an easy natural one,—one that will allow the arm to pass rapidly across the paper without tiring. Some writers prefer holding the pen or pencil between the first and second fingers. Some advantages in shading are to be gained by this position; but it prevents, to some degree, a free action of the hand, and should be used only by those who find that even in very rapid work they can produce equally as good form as with the common long-hand position.

FORMATION OF CHARACTERS.

The student should strive from the beginning to form letters well. The legibility of the New Rapid short-hand depends entirely upon the degree of correctness with which the characters are formed. It is not so particular as to the exact length or size of the characters, so long as the *relative* length or size is preserved. If the short letters are written as in the plates, ⅛ of an inch in length, then the long letters should be correspondingly enough longer to render the two classes perfectly legible.

Each student should write, in some degree at least, such a style as comes natural to his hand. In short-hand the two great points to be gained are speed and legibility; hence, to attain these in the highest degree, first of all the hand-writing executed must be a natural one. Care must be taken, however, not to go to the extremes. If one writes a very large hand, he should try and reduce it a trifle in size, and *vice versa*. The size used in the plates is a medium one, well adapted to all kinds of work; and it will be well for the beginner to copy after this style during his early practice.

It will be observed that the surface characters *b* and *g* are taken from the small letter *n* in long-hand, the *b* being the first part and the *g* the last part. Many other letters can be memorized and written advantageously by associating them with the long-hand alphabet, upon which the system is founded. The *i*, for example, is taken from the first stroke of the *i* in long-hand. Also, the short-hand character for *a* is taken from the first stroke of the *a* in long-hand.

COMBINING LETTERS.

Characters are combined in the easiest, natural manner. Those which require any particular direction were explained on page 39.

The letter *l*, which is similar to a cipher, is generally turned on the preceding or following character. Thus it will be observed that one-half of the letter *l* is already made in forming the stroke on which it is turned. The learner should form the habit of making the *l* very narrow. It can, when thus formed, be written much faster. It is less likely to look like the circle *s*, and presents a neater appearance.

The circle *s* is turned on other characters the same as the *l*. It is turned on the inside of curves, on the left hand side of the descending and ascending straight lines, and on the upper side of the *m* and *n*.

The *sh* and *wh* are taken from a small circle, the *sh* being the left half of the circle and the *wh* the right half. They are joined in an angular manner. (See lines 13 and 14).

COMBINATIONS.

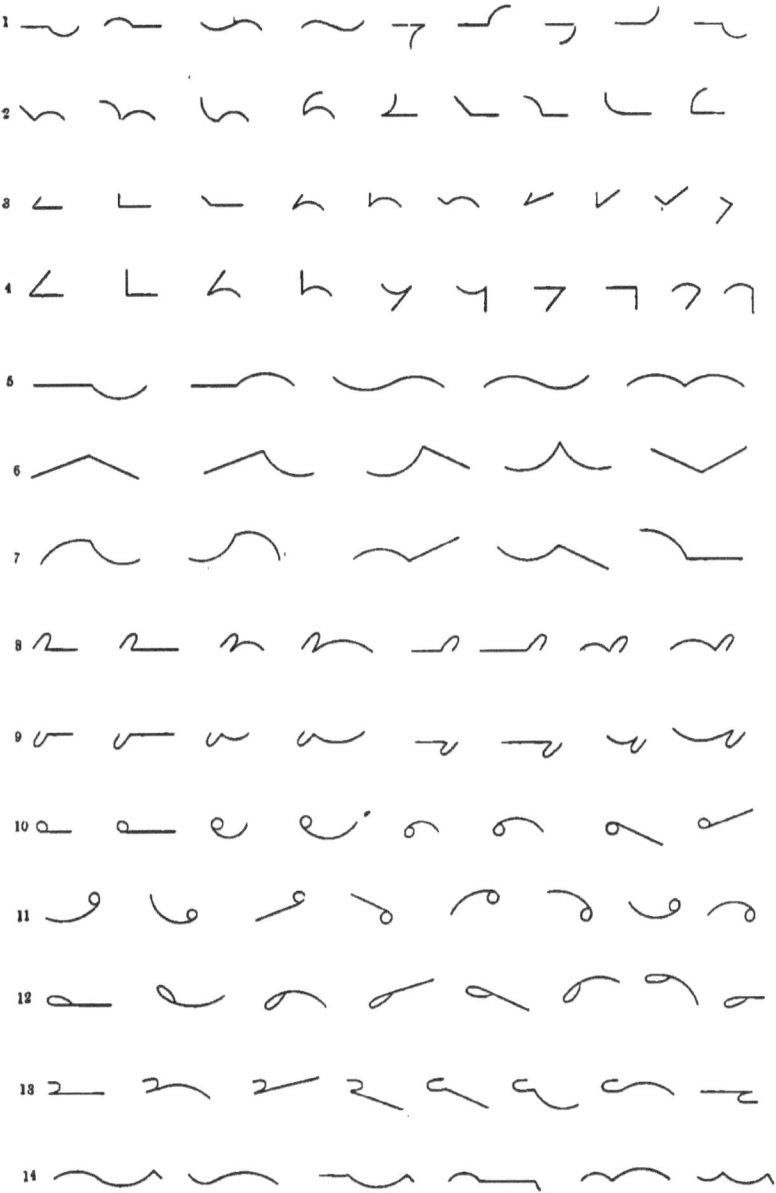

PHONETIC SPELLING.

Phonetic spelling is one of the fundamental principles of short-hand, and means *spelling by sound*. From this will be seen the reason why the alphabet contains more than twenty-six letters; since to spell phonetically it is necessary to have a character to represent all the sounds of the language.

By this method, spelling becomes an easy matter, as words are spelled as pronounced and without regard to the regular orthography. Thus the word *thought* would be written *thot*, *through* would be written *thru*, etc.

The object of short-hand is to secure brevity in writing, and hence it will be seen that the great importance of phonetic spelling lies in the brevity it secures. Thus the word *thought*, which contains seven letters, written phonetically has but four; while the word *through* is correspondingly shortened.

The object then of Phonetic spelling in the writing of short-hand is to secure brevity and simplicity. It is, however, none the less valuable in all the methods of writing and printing. It would be a great blessing to the world at large if Phonetic spelling were in every day use. By it the child could learn to read in one-tenth the time required by the present method. We would experience no difficulty in the pronunciation of words, even at first sight. It would banish provincialisms, and the English language the world over would become uniform in pronunciation and spelling.

The principle of Phonetic spelling, is so simple and easily applied, that it is hardly necessary to give any special rules or

PRINCIPLES.

directions; but since the beginner is very apt to allow the common English spelling to mislead him, in some words, we give a few lists for the purpose of training the ear and eye to a correct knowledge of the sounds contained in words.

RULE I.
OMIT ALL SILENT LETTERS.

CONSONANTS.

1.—Omit one of double letters.

will	wil	letter	letr
kill	kil	little	litl
loss	los	funny	funy
ebb	eb	lesson	lesn
manner	manr	better	betr
matter	matr	ribbon	ribn

2.—Omit t.

often	ofn	pitch	pich
soften	sofn	match	mach
fasten	fasn	kitchen	kichn
listen	lisn	dispatch	dispach

3.—Omit l.

could	kud	half	haf
would	wud	psalm	sam
palm	pam	should	shud
walk	wak	chalk	chak

4.—Omit b.

lamb	lam	plumb	plum
climb	klim	debt	det
thumb	thum	doubt	dout

5.—Omit n.

column	kolm	solemn	solm
hymn	hym	condemn	kondm

6.—Omit c.

back	bak	shock	shŏk
track	trak	quick	quik
sick	sik	rock	rŏk
scent	sent	descend	desend
crescent	kresnt	rescind	resind
muscle	musl	science	siens

7.—Omit gh.

sleigh	sla	weight	wat
taught	taut	might	mit
caught	kaut	sight	sit
daughter	dautr	fright	frit
slaughter	slautr	delight	delit

8.—Omit w.

write	rit	written	ritn
wreck	rek	wrestle	resl
wrong	rong	wrinkle	rinkl
whole	hol	wrangle	rangl
show	sho	throw	thro
snow	sno	flow	flo

9.—Omit k.

knife	nif	know	no
knit	nit	knee	ne
knot	not	knell	nel

10.—Omit g.

gnaw	naw	resign	resin
gnat	nat	design	desin
sign	sin	foreign	forin

VOWELS.

11.—Omit e.

| stole | stol | shine | shin |
| same | sam | fine | fin |

12.—Omit y.

say	sa	lay	la
day	da	stay	stay
they	tha	pray	pra

13.—Omit one of double letters.

see	se	seed	sed
tree	tre	feed	fed
free	fre	sheet	shet

14.—Omit a.

death	deth	boat	bōt
bread	bred	fear	fĕr
earth	erth	beast	bĕst
each	ech	oath	ōth

15.—Omit u.

soul	sol	guild	gild
course	cors	guise	giz
guide	gid	source	sors

16.—Omit i.

faint	fant	hail	hăl
priest	prĕst	sail	săl
saint	sant	mail	măl

SUBSTITUTING.

17.—Substitute u for ew.

new	nu	knew	nu
crew	kru	view	vu
few	fu	strew	stru
flew	flu	review	revu

18.—Substitute z for s where the sound is clearly that of z.

does	duz	size	siz
says	sez	lays	laz
cause	kauz	lies	liz

19.—Substitute s for c when it represents its soft sound.

since	sins	certain	sertn
twice	twis	office	ofis
force	fors	justice	justis

20.—Substitute t for ed, since the sound is that of t.

wished	wisht	finished	finisht
washed	washt	fished	fisht
flashed	flasht	polished	polisht

21.—Substitute j for g and dg.

gem	jem	judge	juj
gentle	jentl	bridge	brij
german	jermn	edge	ej

22.—Substitute q for gu and gw. Since the *u* always follows *q* it is omitted after the *q*.

| languish | lanqsh | distinguish | distinqsh |
| languid | lanqd | anguish | anqsh |

23.—Substitute f for ph when ph has the sound of f.

phonetic	fonetic	philosophy	filosofy
phrase	frase	phonography	fonografy
alphabet	alfabet	phantom	fantom

DIPHTHONGS.

joy	j oy	annoy	an oy
toil	t oi l	alloy	al oy
soil	s oi l	employ	empl oy

how	h ow	flour	fl ou r
now	n ow	loud	l ou d
plow	pl ow	tower	t ow r

POINTS WORTH REMEMBERING.

I. Write the sounds of words and not the letters.

II. Write Vowels whenever they are necessary to secure legibility.

III. Write every word as briefly as is consistent with legibility.

IV. Write such outlines as will best preserve legibility when written at a high rate of speed.

V. Write rapidly from the first but never make a stroke that is not perfectly legible.

VI. Write shaded strokes with one sweep of the pen.

VII. Write derivative words by simply adding to the primitive.

VIII. Write all circles and loops on the inside of curves and on the left side of straight lines.

IX. Write easily, rapidly, legibly, and beautifully.

X. Study earnestly and diligently. Practice intelligently. Persevere or don't attempt.

VOWEL POSITIONS.

Consonants are written on positions so as to express the following vowel. The vowels are assigned positions above and below the base line in their alphabetical order. The middle vowel (*i*) being placed on the base line.

Consonants are always followed by vowels; hence they are written on these positions, to express a following vowel. To write *mi*, we write *m* on the base line, as this is the *i* position. To write *me*, we write *m* just above the base line, as this is the *e* position; and so on through the different positions. It will be observed that the vowel expressed by the position always follows immediately after the first consonant, and that this is the only vowel that is expressed by the position. When more vowels occur in a word they are written, hence, only the first consonant in each word is written on position; those which follow are written without reference to position.

The learner will remember that all silent letters are omitted. Since *y* final has the same sound as *i*, it is placed on the same position. Each position is assigned but one vowel; hence, such words as main and man would be written on the same position. It is seldom necessary to make a distinction between long and short vowels in such words; but, when it is called for, it is done by placing a minute horizontal dash near the word to indicate long sound of the vowel position, and leaving the unmarked stroke to represent short sound. (See line 3).

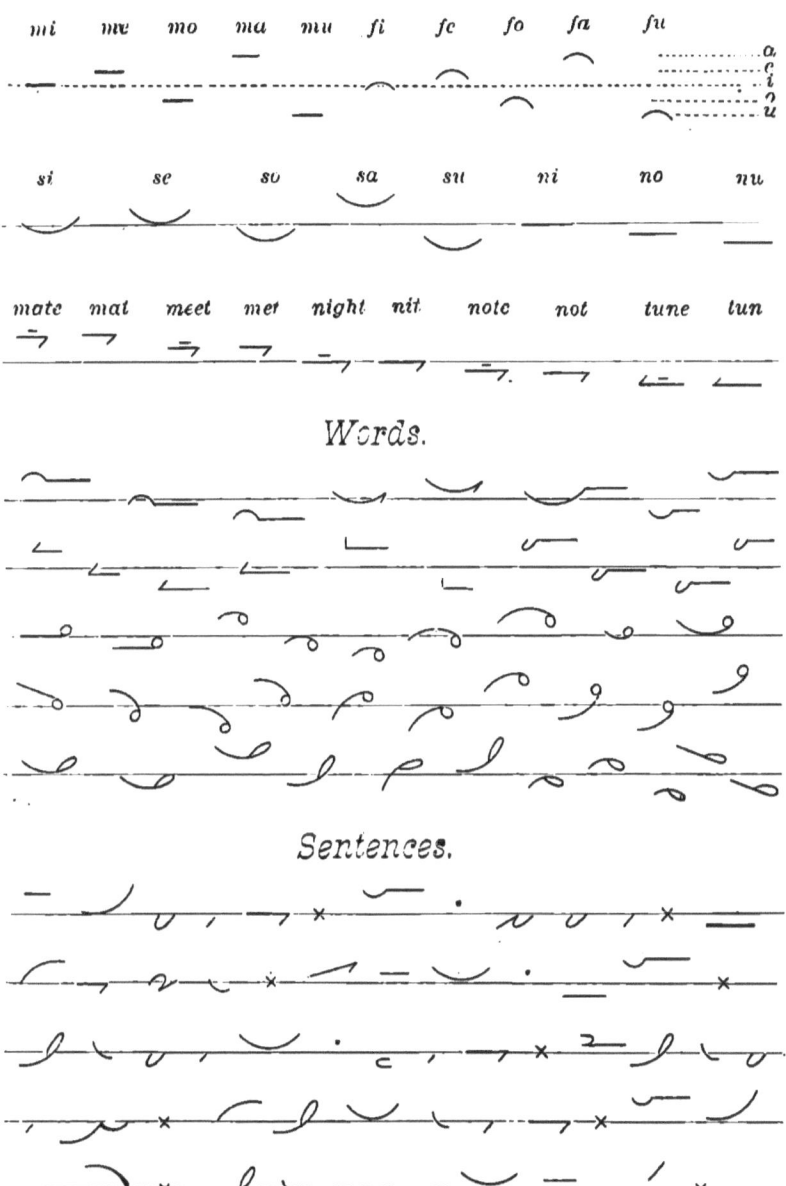

It is not necessary that the positions occupy much space perpendicularly. Owing to the running style of writing produced in this system, strokes can be written close to the base line and yet express each position very legibly.

It will be observed that to write on the *i* position, the characters are placed directly on the line. To write on the *e* or *o* position, they are placed above or below very close to the line; and for the farthest positions *a* and *u*, the characters are written entirely free from the line.

As a rule, beginners are apt to allow the positions to take up too much room. Much time is wasted in moving the hand upward or downward when the positions are scattered. Lineality in writing is one of the chief essentials towards gaining a high rate of speed. Since it is important that the student realizes this from the beginning, and carries it into immediate practice, we have presented the positions from the very first in as close a form as they are used in rapid reporting.

PRINCIPLES.   53

DIPHTHONG POSITIONS.

A Diphthong is a coalition or union of two vowel sounds pronounced in one syllable.

The diphthongs are assigned positions so as to coincide as near as possible with the vowel sounds found on the same position.

They are as follows:— $\begin{matrix} au & aw \\ -- oi & oy -- - \\ ou & ow \end{matrix}$

Words are written on these positions the same as on the vowel positions, but in order to distinguish them apart a dot is used to indicate the diphthongal sound.

The dot is placed anywhere near the character preced ng the diphthongal sound. It will be found after considerable practice in writing and reading that the dot can be omitted in many cases. The outline of the word aided by the context is generally sufficient to render it perfectly legible.

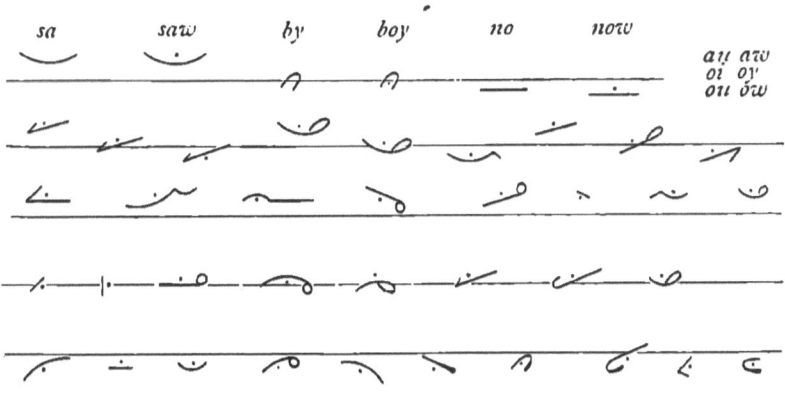

THE *R* RULE.

There are certain consonants with which the *r* unites, forming coalescents. The prime object of using the principle of shading for *r* is to write these coalescents with one stroke. Hence they are shaded to indicate the immediate presence of an *r*, forming such words as pray, free, try, etc. This secures two letters in one stroke which is written on position to express the following vowel. (See line 2.)

Since *r* coalesces only with the letters *f, t, d, p, k, g, b, th* and *sh*, and is expressed by a shade near the center, the writer can, if he chooses, shade the beginning of a stroke to prefix *r*, and the end to add *r*. When *r* precedes or follows a long stroke, as in rise, rain, pair, there, etc., it will be found very advantageous to express it in this manner.

This system, as compared with others, makes very little use of shading. When shades are used, however, they play an important part, and it is well that the student at the very outset learn to write and read them readily. Beginners invariably shade too heavy. It is not necessary that shaded strokes be very thick. In writing with a pencil, which most writers use, it is sufficient to simply impart to it a darker hue by a light increase of pressure. The student should practice considerably, reading and writing light shaded strokes. In no case should shades be formed by retracing. The student should remember that in short-hand all strokes must be formed so that they can be written at a high rate of speed, and hence must always be written with one sweep of the pen. When *r* is not a coalescent it is generally best to employ the tick.

THE *R* RULE.

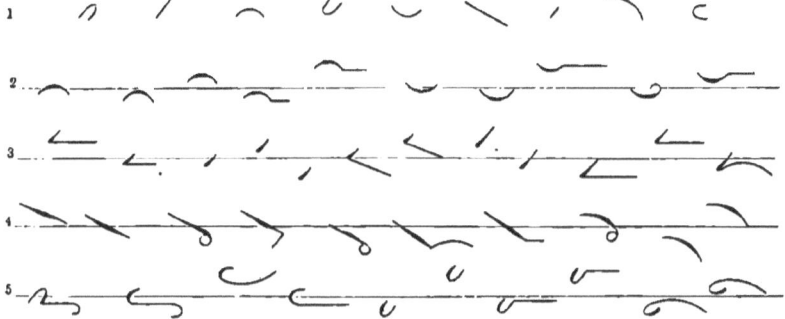

Words written from the principle of Coalescent *r*.

Tray, tree, try, trow, train, trim, trill, trail, trade, treat, trait, trod, trot, dray, dry, drum, drag, drug, dragging, chain, dress, drift, draft, free, fry, fro, frame, from, fruit, freight, fraught, bridge, brush, brook, brought, bring, braid, grade, greed, grind, grow, grown, grain, gruff, cry, crew, crow, crude, cried, crush, crumb, crimp, cringe, crave, pray, pry, price, proud, proof, prate, print, prove, three, threw, through, thrice, shrine, shred, shrink, shroud, drudge, drug, crash, crash, crank, crisp, cross, crowd, crust, breast, broil, brother, preach, preside, principal, prostrate, prudent.

HOOK LETTERS.

The hook letters *b* and *g* are turned on the character to which they are attached as a continuation. *b* is turned on the upper side, (see line 1); *g* is turned on the under side, (see line 2.)

These letters are turned as hooks for the purpose of facilitating joinings and rendering the writing easier in execution. Sometimes, however, they are joined in their natural alphabetical form.

The writer should always use whichever is formed the easiest and best adapted to the purpose. These hooks do not in any way conflict with the *sh* and *wh* since the latter are joined in an angular manner. (See line 11.) For reasons which will be apparent to the learner further along, it is desirble to have a similar method of representing their cognates *p* and *k*. This is accomplished by using a shorter hook on the upper side to represent the *p* and on the lower side for the *k*. (See lines 7 and 8.)

The *p* and *k* being so closely allied in sound to the *b* and *g* it is not necessary that any great difference be made. More than one half the systems in use make no difference whatever between cognates. This system however, preserves a distinction in all cases.

PRINCIPLES. 57

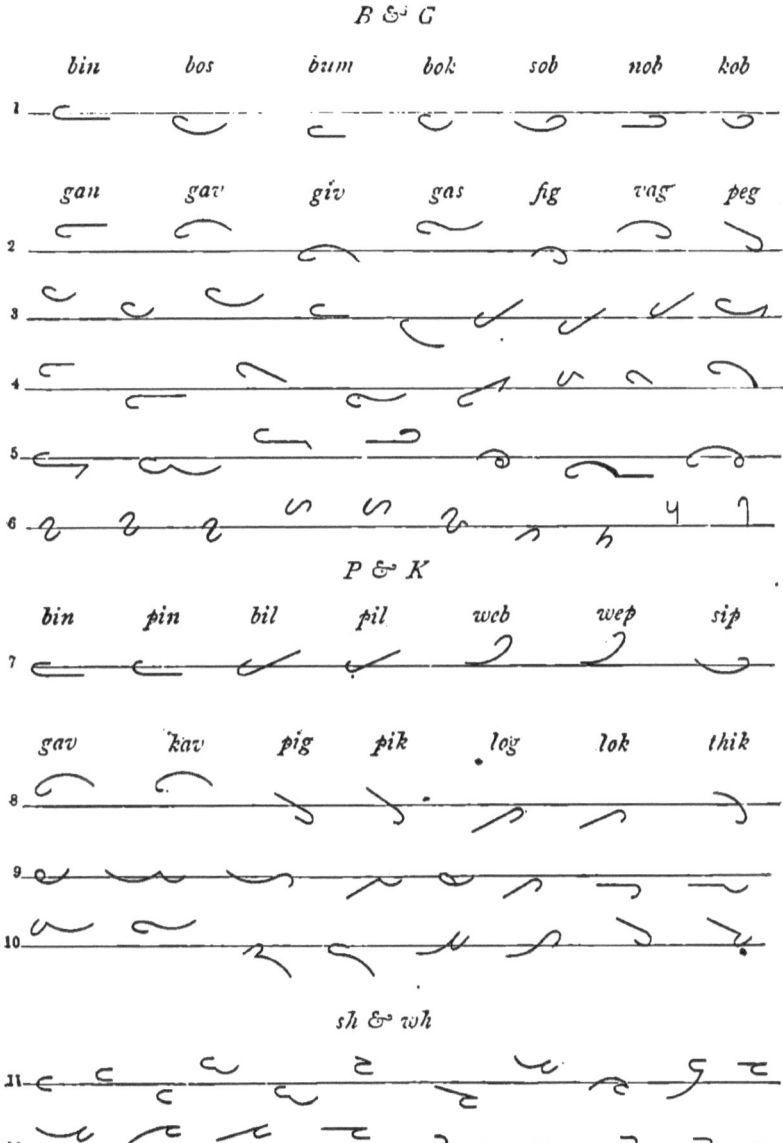

WORD SIGNS.

The principles of this system secure such a remarkable degree of brevity in writing that word-signs are almost entirely done away with. It would be possible to dispense with them entirely, but since there are a few words that occur very frequently, and which if written out in full would require two strokes, it is found expedient to omit one of the letters, and express them by a single stroke.

To the right will be found a complete list of the word-signs, which should be thoroughly memorized. These word-signs which are accompanied by dotted lines are written on the position indicated by the line. Those without lines are written irregardless of position.

The dot is written on four different positions; on *a* position for *ah*; on *e* position for the word *the*; on *i* position for *I*; and on *o* position for *oh*, and *owe*.

The vowel stroke for *u* is used for the word *you* which is written irregardless of position.

It is shaded for the word *your*.

WORD SIGNS.

The	.	Which	—|—	Of	⌐
I	•	Church	___	All	0
Are	`	Judge	·|	After	(
As	°	If	⌒	Any	`
Is	°.	Have	⌒	Every	⌐

SENTENCES.

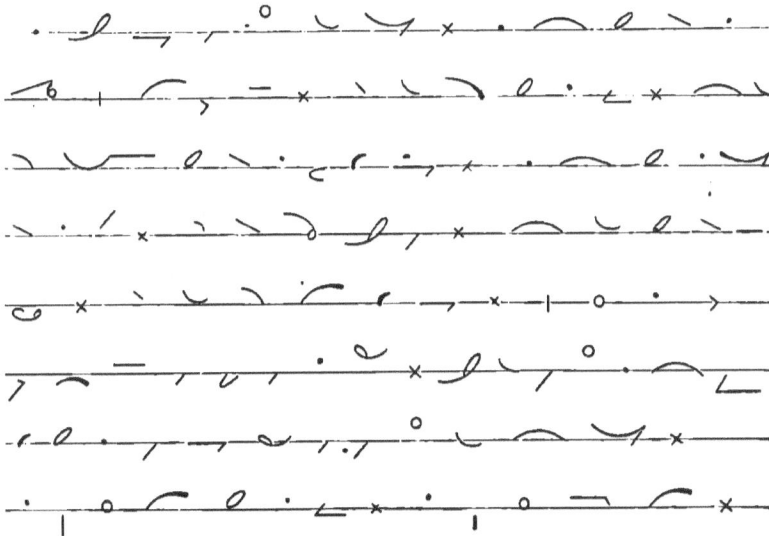

SENTENCES.

He *would* not take *any after all.* We *all* go to *the* new *church.* *I have your* hat *and* cane. *You* can come *after it.* *Which would you have* done? *Which* one *are you after?* We *were at the church after* dark. *If I had all* that *you could* give.

Can you come soon? When can you send him home? The man went with them to find some one. The same man won the race. He gave them all the honor. I knew you went with them. Give the reason why you can not do it. I want that long line. Since when can you find them. I think you might have given them to me. Have you been with them long? When do you think they could send him some?

REVIEW QUESTIONS.

What are the two fundamental principles of short-hand?
Why are curves elliptical instead of circular?
What advantages, if any, are to be gained by writing a small hand?
How are the *l* and *s* united with curved strokes? On which side of straight lines are they turned?
In what way can the *r* and another letter be expressed in one stroke?
How is the *r* written before another letter, expressing both in one stroke? How is it written after another character, expressing both in one stroke?
What is Phonetic spelling? What are the advantages to be gained by spelling phonetically?
How many vowel positions are there? How distinguish long vowel sounds from the short when writing on position?
How many word-signs are there? Name them. What ones are written irregardless of position? How many of the word-signs are shaded strokes?
How is *b* turned on other characters as a hook? On what side is *g* turned as a hook? What does the hook on the upper side represent, when written a trifle shorter? What the hook on the lower side? How do you distinguish these hooks when turned on other letters from *sh* and *wh*?
How many sounds are there in the word *taught?* How would this word be written?
In writing with a pen how should it be held in order to shade strokes without a change of position?
How often should the Plate exercises be written and read?

The foregoing principles will enable one to write the English language in full at least four times as fast as can be done with common long-hand. But in order to write as rapidly as one speaks, it must be capable of being written about six times as fast as long-hand. The principles which follow are for the purpose of securing brevity and increasing speed. They are few and simple, but of great importance, and must be thoroughly mastered.

The first principle made use of is the lengthening of long characters.

PRINCIPLE FIRST.

The long characters and hook letters *b*, *g*, *sh* and *wh* are lengthened to add *m* or *n*.

In lengthening these characters care should be taken to add simply enough in length to render them perfectly legible. About one-third longer than the normal size is sufficient. It will be observed that the vowel expressed by the position continues to follow immediately after the first consonant; and hence the added *m* or *n* is always read after the vowel.

In permitting the characters to undergo these different changes, it is necessary that the relative sizes be preserved.

In such words as simon, lemon, etc., the final *n* blends so closely with the *m*, that it is desirable to express it by a similar principle. Therefore long letters are superlengthened to add *mn*. (See lines 13 and 14). To superlengthen a stroke, it is made double the alphabet length.

PRINCIPLES. 63

LONG LETTERS.

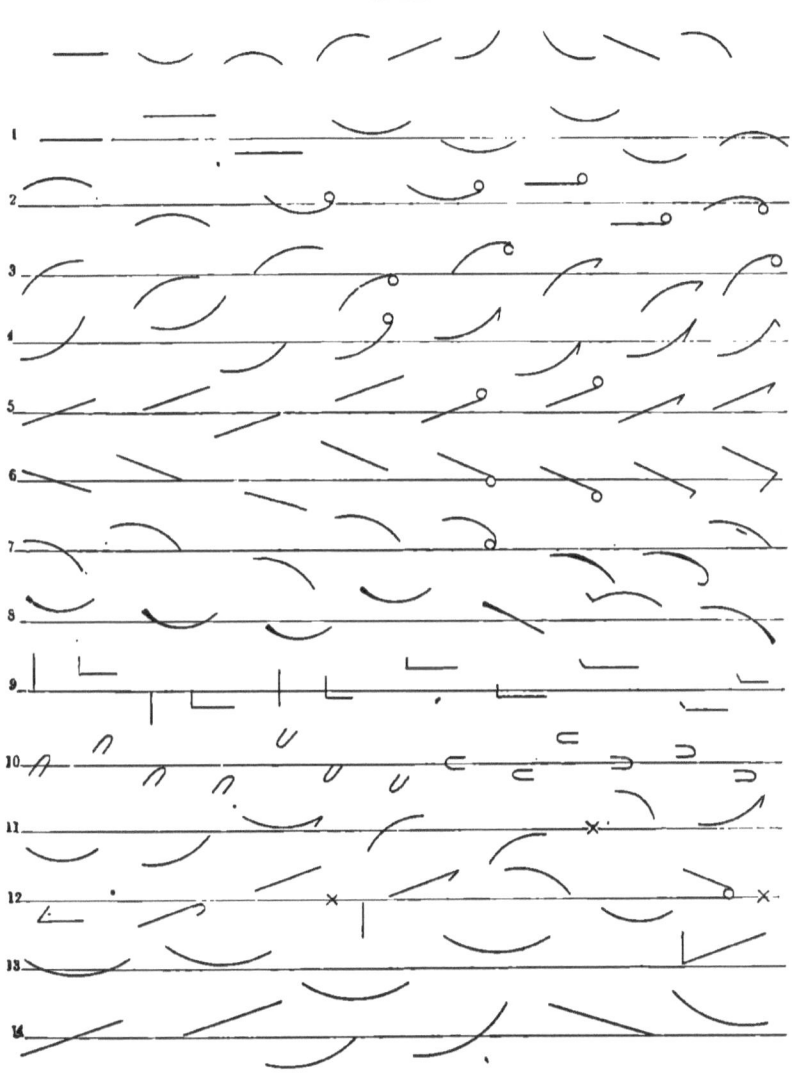

Words Written by the Lengthening Principle.

Name, nine, noon, nun, names, same, seem, sin, soon, sun, seems, summer, sinner, van, vine, vum, home, hum, him, hem, ham, homes, hammer, lame, lane, lean, line, lone, lanes, lines, limbs, wine, wun, wines, want, went, wind, winner, pan, pen, pin, pun, paint, pint, pond, pens, pannel, them, than, thin, thumb, Jane, John, Jim, June, Genesee, reason, raisin, risen, rosen, ripen, raven, gain, gone, gun, gum, begin, begun, been, bun, banner, shame, shine, shone, shun, when, whim, whine, whom.

SENTENCES.

John sent him nine pens this winter.
Since when did they send them?
Is that the reason why Simon went home then?
What do you think he will send?
This is the gentleman to whom you lent nine dollars last summer.
How long do you think it will take him?
The gentleman whom you sent after these pens is a fine penman.
Have you seen John's new pen?
This long line which I have was sent to James.
I will send him some of these since he was so kind to me.

REVIEW QUESTIONS.

Does the added *m* or *n* come before or after the vowel position.

How many different classes of letters are there?

For what are long letters lengthened? Superlengthened?

How much longer than the regular length should a stroke be made to express *m* or *n*? To express *mn*?

Is *j* a long letter? Can it be lengthened to express *m* or *n*?

How do you express the *r* in such words as *reason, risen, ripen, rack*, etc.? What surface characters are lengthened to add *m* or *n*?

PRINCIPLE SECOND.

SHORT CHARACTERS SHORTENED TO ADD *m* OR *n*.

Most of the short characters are vowels, and hence words in which these occur are written on position to express the next vowel in the word. Thus, to write the word invent, we write minute *i* which expresses the *n*, and then write long *v* on the *e* position adding the *t*. Words in which the only vowel is initial, such as *in*, *it*, *an*, *on*, etc., are written regardless of position.

The *r*, *t* and *ch* are minute ticks and are never changed in length.

Since the *t* and *d* are generally drawn downwards, we take advantage of their reversible nature and strike them upwards to add *m* or *n*. (See lines 6, 7 and 8).

The words *in*, *an* and *on* are written from this principle, regardless of position.

PRINCIPLES. 67

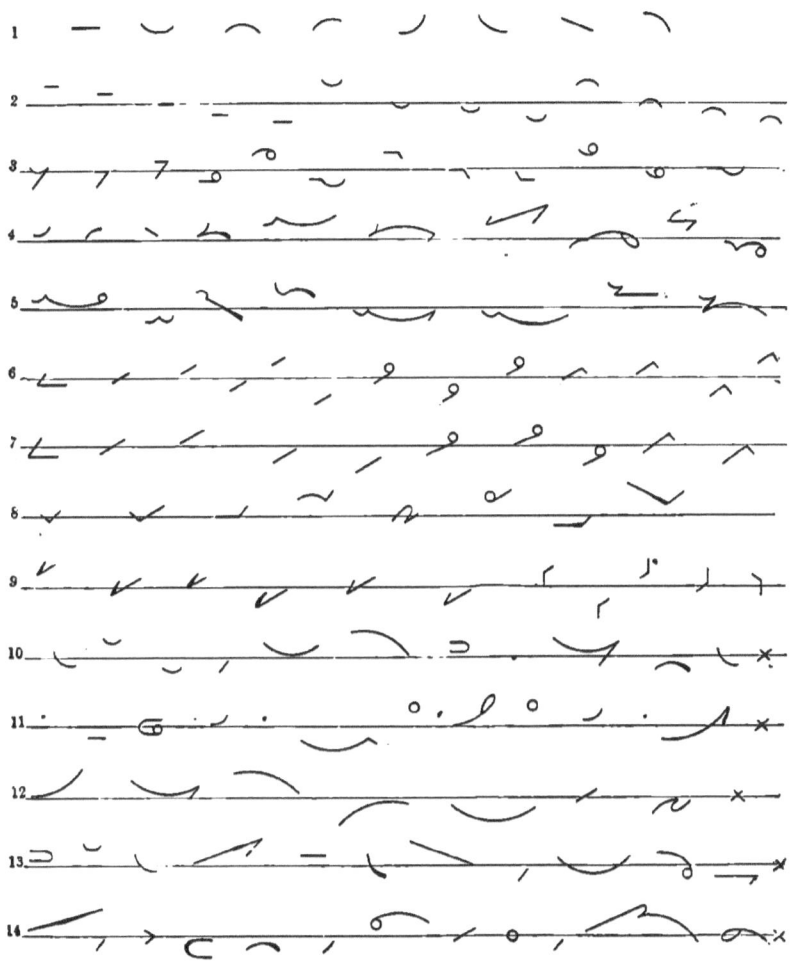

WORDS WRITTEN BY THE SHORTENING PRINCIPLE.

Man, main, men, mean, moon, mum, mens, moons, manner, miner, kind, cans, comes, mankind, fan, find, foam, fun, fans, invent, insane, income, inland, infer, inmate, tame, teem, time, tune, times, tunes tanner, tuner, dame, dum, dine, done, dimes, domes, dinner, tied, tried, treat.

SENTENCES.

The man went down town after his dinner.
Can't you give me ten times as much?
In an hour or two he will come.
The man was no doubt insane.
Can you teach him to write next winter?
Can I see him in time to go down there before noon?
I can now write ten times as fast as I could.

REVIEW QUESTIONS.

What letter or letters is added to *T* and *D* when written upwards.

Does this principle apply in such words as *treat, tread, tried*, etc?

For what are short letters made half length?

What are the tick letters? Are they ever changed in length?

What three small words are written regardless of position?

How do we know the direction in which *t* and *d* are written when standing alone.

PRINCIPLE THIRD.

The surface characters *b*, *g*, *sh*, *wh*, *l* and *s* are enlarged to add *t* or *d*.

It may appear to the learner as being rather indefinite to allow either *t* or *d* to be expressed or as in the preceding lesson *m* or *n*. But after a little experience in writing and reading it will be found that there are very few cases where the same outline will produce words that are liable to conflict. When such words do arise, however, the writer should not hesitate to add *t* or *d* or any other letter when legibility requires it.

This system, as compared to others, is very free from representing different words with the same outline. It will be observed that what few are written alike are those that are almost identical in pronunciation.

The learner should exercise the same care in enlarging these characters proportionally as in the writing of the long and short letters.

The circle *s* enlarged adds *t*, making the coalescent *st* which is written on position for the following vowel. (See line 7). On other surface characters the expressed *t* or *d* always follows after the vowel position.

The surface character *l* does not stand alone since it is used for the word all. To write the words *lay, lie, low*, etc., the long *l* is employed.

PRINCIPLES.

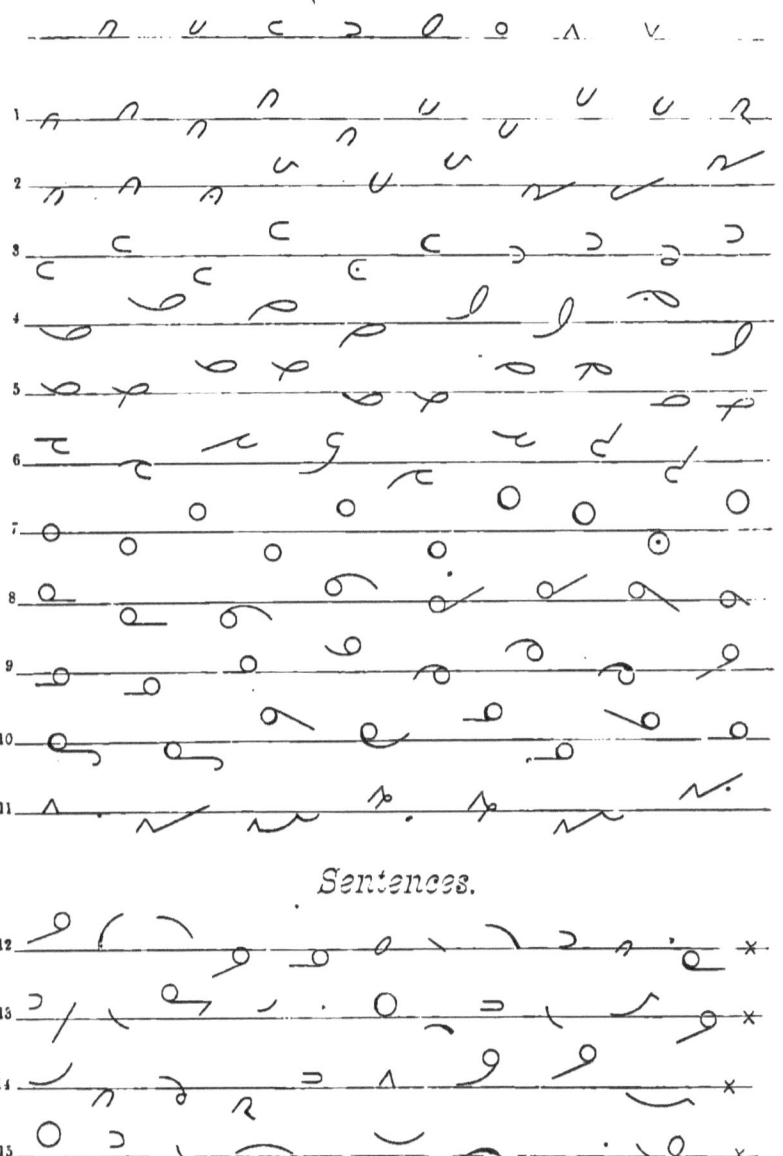

Sentences.

Words Written by the Enlarging Principle.

Bat, bet, bed, bit, bid, bought, but, better, bitter, butter, gate, get, guide, good, gaiter, shade, shed, shut, should, white, what, wheat, sold, sailed, hold, held, halt, wild, wield, piled, called, cold, killed, stain, stem, stone, stun, stove, stave, star, stir, stop, steep, stole, stale, still, steal, sticks, most, mist, mast, must, fast, fist, feast, cast, coast, vast, vest, west, host, waste, hast, last, least, lost, past, post, just, jest, out, outwork, outline.

REVIEW QUESTIONS.

III. What are the surface characters? How many are there? Name them. For what are they enlarged? Does the expressed *t* or *d* follow immediately after the consonant or the vowel position? How in the case of large *s*? How write such words as *lad, led* and *lit*?

How write such words as, stale, stood, and straight.

SENTENCES WRITTEN BY THE ENLARGING PRINCIPLE.

It is better to be good than to be great.
The butter was lost or stolen.
They were almost wild over the last storm.
The colt stepped on the bat and killed it.
We stopped and looked on the vast mountain of stone.
They sailed up Salt river last June.
Peter was a great and good man.
I thought the bat was a night bird.
We bought a better boat.
He was brought here after night.
You should not stop so soon.
How short the winter is out west.
You should be good no matter what happens.

PRINCIPLE FOURTH.

SURFACE CHARACTERS DIMINISHED TO ADD *l*.

The learner will doubtless understand now why the *b* and *g* are represented by surface characters, and also the importance of having a similar way of expressing the *p* and *k*. The letter *l* unites with these consonants forming the coalescents *bl*, *gl*, *pl*, *kl*, *fl* and *sl*. The initial letters being represented by surface characters, they are simply written a trifle smaller to add the *l*, thus expressing them both with one small character. (See lines 1, 2 and 3). It will be observed that the expressed *l* always follows after the consonant. When a vowel intervenes, as in gale, bale, etc., both consonants are written.

Should the learner experience any difficulty in reading his writing, to distinguish the *pl* from the *bl* or the *kl* from the *gl*, he can use the *b* and *g* in their alphabetic form, *i. e.*, joining them in an angular manner, and express the *p* and *k* by the turned hooks. (See line 10).

The *s* is diminished to add *l* only when medial and final. (See line 13). The writing of initial coalescent *sl* comes under the "*s*" coalescents which will be explained in a following lesson.

The *l* diminished makes *f* precede instead of adding *l*, thus writing all of the *l* coalescents by the diminishing principle.

The *sh* and *wh* being surface characters, also come under this diminishing rule; but since the *l* never unites with them, forming coalescents, they are written on position to express the intervening vowel, making the words *sh a ll*, *wh i le*, etc.

The diphthongs being surface characters are also diminished to add *l*.

PRINCIPLES.

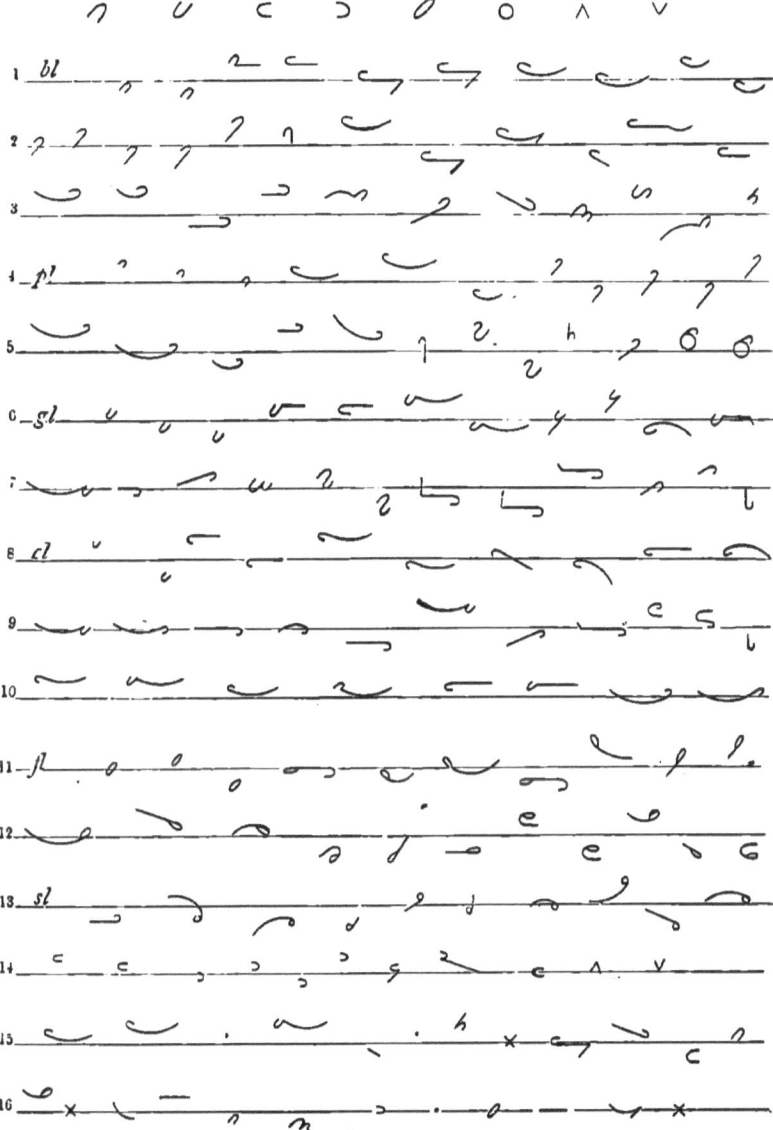

Words Written from the Diminishing Principle of Surface Characters.

Blue, blow, blame, bloom, bless, bliss, blade, bleat, blind, blend, blond, fable, Mable, noble, nimble, sable, symbol, thimble, pebble, lable, lible, cable, bible, bubble, gabble, bleach, blush, plain, place, please, plus, pledge, plead, plod, plight, pluck, plate, plot, play, ply, sample, couple, people, example, steeple, staple, apple, chapel, glue, glow, glean, glimmer, glad, glide, gland, glass, gloss, glove, mingle, single, giggle, goggles, dangle, wrangle, wiggle, tingle, clay, clue, claim, climb, clan, clown, class, close, clip, cleave, clove, cloth, clear, club, clog, sickle, nickle, knuckle, chuckle, pickle, fickle, tackle, oil.

REVIEW QUESTIONS.

For what are surface characters diminished? What is the difference between *pl* and *bl*? How write the coalescent *fl*? What is the difference between the writing of the words *pale* and *play*? How write the coalescent *sl*? With how many letters does *l* coalesce? Can the diphthongs be diminished to add *l*?

SENTENCES WRITTEN BY THE DIMINISHING PRINCIPLE.

It was a splendid place to play.
We found the place plain and pleasant.
There is a deep plot in the play.
Beautiful plates of brass were seen.
Please lay the thimble on the table.
The flame flashed fearfully.
The beautiful bird flew into the flame and was killed.
The delightful glow and glimmer of the summer sun.
The clown pleased the people.

COALESCENT *S*.

This letter unites with *n, m, p, k, t, l, q, f* and *w*. Unlike the coalescent *r* and *l*, it comes first, coalescing with the following letter forming such words as *smile*, *spy*, *stain*, etc.

In order that these coalescents may be written, as the *l* and *r*, from a principle universal in its application, we turn the circle very small on the letter with which *s* unites as a coalescent.

When *s* coalesces with a consonant at the end of a word, as in desk, wisp, etc., each letter forming the coalescent is written in its natural form.

The triplets *spl* and *spr* are written from the same principle, *s* being turned on *pl* for *spl*, and on the *pr* for *spr*. (See line 9).

The circle for coalescent *s* should be very small. If it is so small as to practically result in a dot, it will be found equally as legible, and less likely to conflict with the natural form of *s*.

PRINCIPLES.

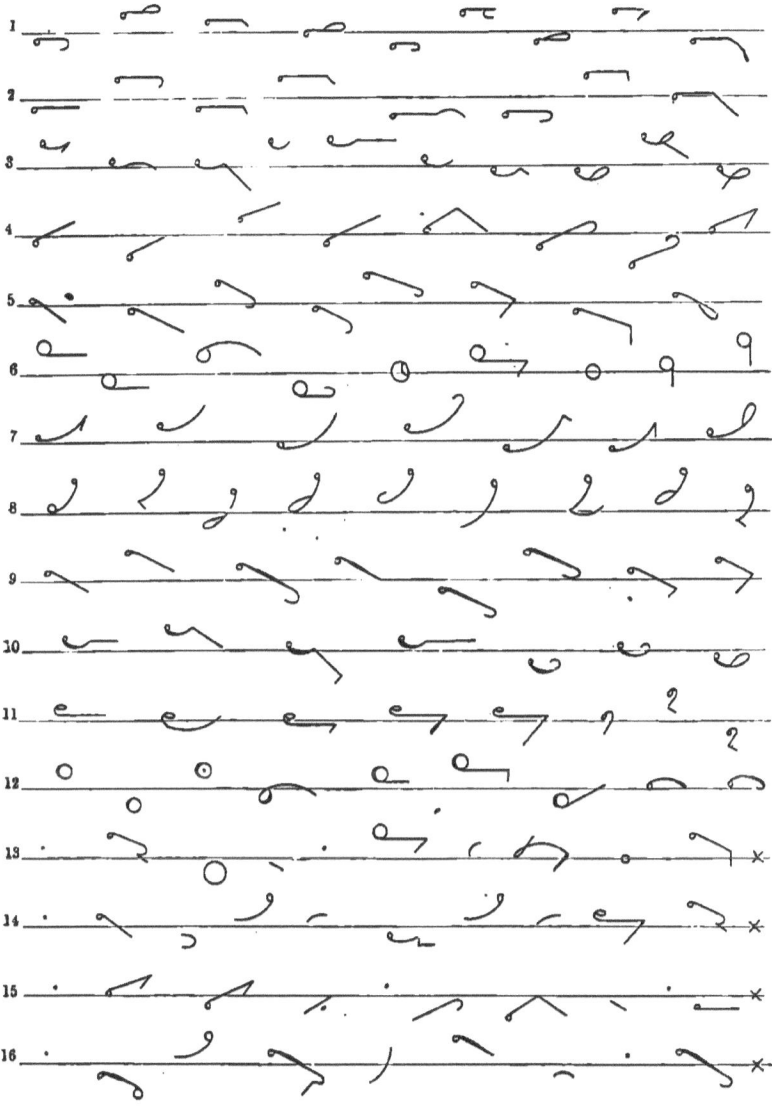

WORDS WRITTEN FROM THE PRINCIPLE OF COALESCENT *s*.

Skate, sketch, skiff, skill, skim, skimming, skip, skipper, skull, sky, scale, scalp, scan, scandal, scant, scape, scheme, school, school-house, scold, score, scowl, scramble, scrape, scream, screen, scribble, scrub, script, slain, slim, slander, slant, slate, slaughter, sled, sledge, sleep, sleigh, slide, slight, sling, slip, slipper, slope, sloth, slouch, slowly, sluggard, slumber, slush, small, smart, smash, smear, smell, smile, smith, smoke, smooth, smother, smuggle, smoulder, snail, snake, snap, snare, snarl, snatch, sneak, sneer, sneeze, snipe, snore, snow, snub, snuff, snug, snugly.

Spy, space, span, spangle, spanish, spar, sparkle, spasm, speak, spear, special, specimen, speckle, speculation, speech, speed, spell, spend, spike, spindle, spine, spinning, spirit, spiritual, splendor, spleen, splash, splice, splint, splinter, split, splutter, sponge, spoon, spoonful, sport, spot, spout, sprain, sprang, spray, spread, spree, spright, spring, sprout, sprinkle, spruce, sprung, squab, squabble, squall, square, squash, squeak, squeeze, squint, squirm, squirrel, stain, steam, stone, stack, staff, stage, stagger, stale, stall, stamp, stanch, stand, standard, standing, staple, star, starch, starlight, start, starve, state-room, statesman, station, statistics, stump, stumble, stupid, style, stylish, statute, stead, instead, steal, steam, steamship, steep, steeple, steer, stencil, stenographer, step, stern, stick, stifle, stile, stimulation, sting, stipple, stir, stitch, stock, stoop, store, stout, strain, straight, stranger, straw, streak, stream, street, strength, stride, strike, string, strive, stroll, struck, strong, struggle, strung, sphere, sphinx, spherical, suation, suasive, swamp, swan, swarm, sway, swear, sweat, sweep, sweet, sweel, swift, swim, swimmer, swindle, swing, switch.

REVIEW QUESTIONS.

With how many letters does the letter *s* coalesce?

How are the triplets *spr* and *spl* written?

What is the difference between the writing of the words *spy* and *sip?*

Is the coalescent *st* written from this principle?

How is the triplet *str* written?

Does it matter how small the *s* circle is made for the coalescents?

What sound has the *u* in the words *suation,* and *suasive.*

THE DOWNWARD PRINCIPLE.

Since there are no perpendicular curves and all slanting letters, excepting *y* and *q*, are written to the right in a running manner, they can be written downwards and more uprightly, which is done to add a *t* or *d*.

This principle gives the vowels a wonderful writing power, as they are so frequently followed by *t* and *d*.

The *h* and *w* are seldom written downwards owing to their likeness to the *y* and *q* when so written. The frequent occuring words, *had, heard, would,* and *word,* and the ending *ward* are about the only ones in which the downward principle is applied to the *h* and *w*.

The prefixes *inter, enter,* and *under* are all written from this principle without reference to position. (See lines 9, 10 and 11.)

The shade is omitted in the word *herewith* and written by simply a downward compound curve. (See line 14.)

The shade is also omitted in the word *children.* (See line 11.)

The *w* in the word *with* can be struck either upwards or downwards.

THE DOWNWARD PRINCIPLE.

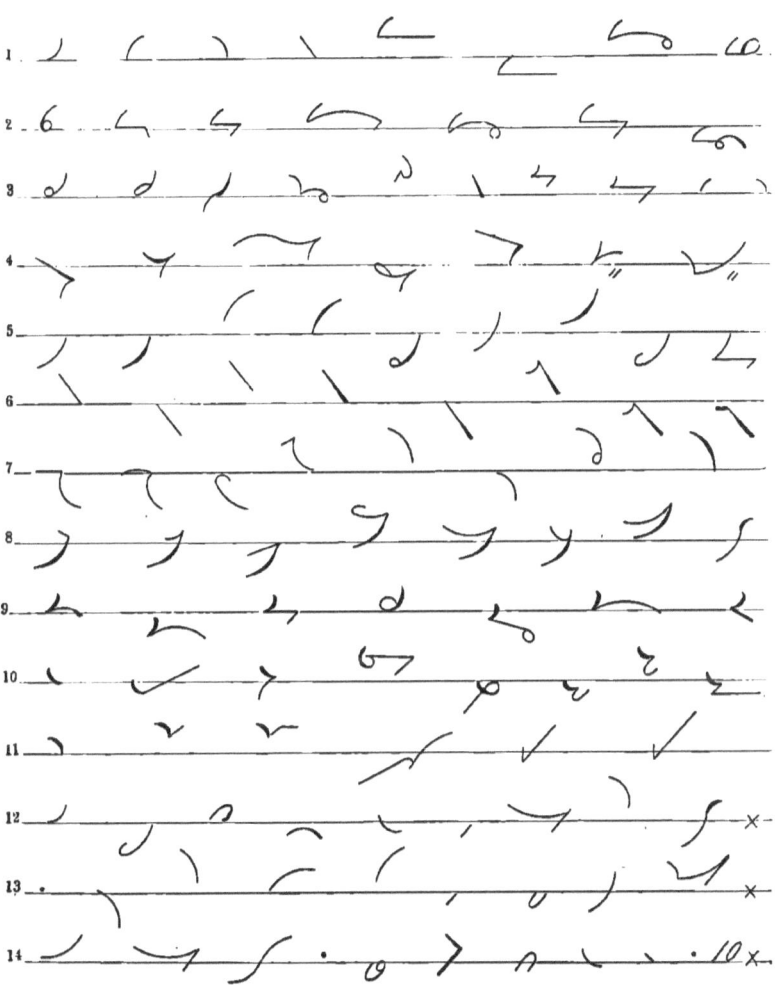

REVIEW QUESTIONS.

ON THE DOWNWARD PRINCIPLE.

What class of characters are written downward to add *t* or *d*?

In what words are the *h* and *w* written downwards?

Why not always write them downwards when followed by *t* and *d*.

How is the phrase *would be* written?

Is the word *and* written on any particular position?

Should *it is* and *it will* be phrased?

How write the words *enter* and *under?*

Are they written on any particular position?

How is the *d* expressed in the word *children*?

How is the word *herewith* written?

In what two words is the shade omitted?

MISCELLANEOUS WORDS AND SENTENCES FOR PRACTICE.

I O a of to in is it he be by or as at we my on ye me no us go an if do
The and for are but all not thy our God you will had see full out his this who can how man may has won now yes .
That with from have they more theirs them there shall thou will upon word Lord when great other were been part truth every world most where time give after first come under work like your ever unto into thee which what those would state very some where make think people dear sir never write words love over place believe because pleasure president amount business between chairmen another thought human knowledge particular

How little we think of the happiness of others in this world.

Live as though you were to die to-morrow; learn as though you were to live forever.

Think twice before you speak and you will have less to regret every day of your life.

Let those keep silence who can speak no good.

What is worth doing at all, is worth doing well?

To succeed in life you must understand and mind your own business.

Seek not after those things of this world which are here to-day but gone to-morrow.

EXPEDIENT PRINCIPLES.

Since the *s* circle is always turned on the regular side of strokes, we make use of the irregular side to express *ts* or *ds*, that is, *s* circle turned on the irregular side makes *t* or *d* precede. (See lines 1, 2 and 3).

s initial on the irregular side expresses the common prefix *dis*. (See lines 4 and 5).

The same rule applies to the *l* which is turned on the irregular side for *tl* and *dl*. (See lines 6, 7 and 8).

Characters are retraced for *Th*. (See line 9).

The retracing is shaded for *r*. (See line 10).

When the retracing does not write easily the stroke is used. (See line 11).

b is joined in an angular manner for the syllable *b*e and the word written on position to express the next vowel. (See line 12).

The *l* is written in a perpendicular manner to express *j*.

The *b* and *g* can also be written upright for the same purpose. (See line 14).

The *l*, *b* and *g* are sloped backwards to add *sh*. (See line 15).

PRINCIPLES. 87

EXPEDIENT PRINCIPLES.

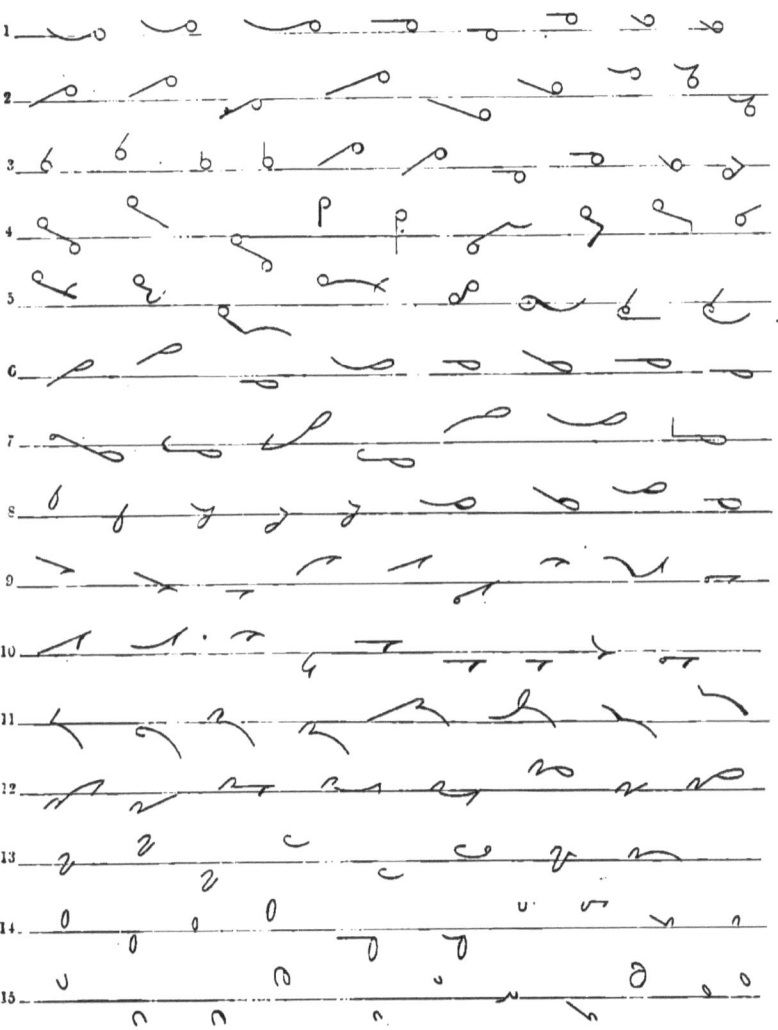

REVIEW QUESTIONS.

ON THE EXPEDIENT PRINCIPLES.

What is the regular side of curved strokes? What is the regular side of straight lines? What is the regular side of *m* and *n* ?

For what is the circle *s* turned on the irregular side initially? What finally?

Is the *l* ever written on the irregular side?

How is *th* expressed when the stroke will not join well?

How would you write the word *farther* and *further* ?

For what is *l* written in a perpendicular manner? Are *b* and *g* ever written in this manner?

When are the *b*, *g* and *l* sloped backwards.

How would you write the word *flash* ?

For what is *b* joined in an angular manner initially?

How write the words, *because*, *became* and *become* ?

Ans.—By turning the *b* on the upper side as a hook.

Are these three words exceptions to the general rule?

SUGGESTIONS ON OUTLINING WORDS.

One of the most essential things in connection with the mastery of short-hand is securing outlines that are legible, uniform in formation, and easy to write. It is possible for a great many words to be written in different ways, and in some cases with a beginner it may be a question as to which is the best outline to adopt.

There are three general laws to be observed in the outlining of every word. First, that of *legibility;* second, *etymological relation;* and third, *simplicity of outline.* Every word which the student outlines himself should first be tested by outlining it in accordance with these three laws, and then adopting the best form, every thing being considered.

Legibility should always be considered first, for without this the other qualities though existing in their highest degree, have no value whatever.

Second, the preserving of anology should be considered in the writing of all words, by treating them as either primitive or derivative, and forming the outlines so as to preserve harmony through all the etymological relations.

The third test to be made, is to see that the outline is one that can be executed easily and is of such mechanical formation as will not deteriorate in rapid writing.

These three laws upon which rests all that is practicable in short-hand writing are interwoven into every principle of the system, and it is these ever-existing powers that makes this system so legible, philosophical and easy in formation.

The student should be careful not to practice on miscellaneous matter outside of the text book until he has thoroughly mastered all the principles of the system. By strictly observing this he will not be troubled with unlearning long alphabetical outlines when new principles are explained and approved outlines given.

THE "Y" ENDINGS.

On the right hand page is given a full list of the different *y* endings. The *y* is expressed by the *i* which is written either upwards or downwards. (See line 1).

Ty and *dy* are expressed by a short *i* or in other words it is the *t* curved slightly. (See line 3).

The *y* is added after any circle or loop by allowing the line to pass over the stem. (See lines 5, 6, 7 and 8).

In the endings *by* and *bly* the *i* is joined in a continuous manner without an angle. (See lines 9 and 10).

The difference between *bly* and *blty* is in the length of the *i*. (See lines 10 and 11)

The *i* is omitted in the ending *fy* and the *f* is increased in curvature slightly to express final *i* or *y*. (See line 12).

The *ing* endings occupy lines 13, 14, 15 and 16.

In these endings the detached character is written on a line with the preceding stroke.

The *l* is written in a horizontal manner for *ingly*.

PRINCIPLES.

THE "Y" ENDINGS.

ENDINGS.	ILLUSTRATIONS.
1 *y*	
2 *ty*	
3 *ty dy*	
4 *try*	
5 *sy*	
6 *sty*	
7 *ly*	
8 *fly*	
9 *by*	
10 *bly ply*	
11 *blty*	
12 *fy*	
13 *ing thing*	
14 *ings things*	
15 *ington*	
16 *ingly*	

REVIEW QUESTIONS.

ON THE *y* ENDINGS.

What is the difference between the endings *y* and *ty* ?
Is there any difference between *ty* and *dy* ?
How is *y* expressed after a circle or loop?
How is it expressed after *b* and *bl*?
What is the difference between *bly* and *blty* ?
How write *fy* ?
What is the difference between *ing* and *ington* ?
How is the *l* written in *ingly* ?
What is the relative position of the *ing* endings?

Words ending in *y*.

foamy	enemy	slimy	palmy	gummy
mumm	economy	astronomy	bloomy	army
stormy	company	botany	progeny	rainy
shiny	tiny	mutiny	tyranny	Jenny
penny	bonny	sunny	bony	felony
colony	ceremony	matrimony	testimony	harmony
stony	thorny	puny	downy	tiny

Words ending in *ry*.

chicanery	scenery	machinery	millinery	nunnery
drapery	slippery	nursery	slavery	knavery
bravery	thievery	revery	roguery	livery
delivery	silvery	query	bowery	dowery
showery	flowery	belfry	dairy	fairy
hairy	miry	inquiry	cavalry	chivalry
rivalry	hostelry	revelry	yeomanry	sultanry
captainry	canonry	masonry	blazonry	theory
gory	allegory	category	glory	memory
armory				

Words ending in *sy*.

easy	greasy	apostasy	heresy	courtesy
daisy	noisy	palsy	flimsy	clumsy
pansy	tansy	quinsy	posy	rosy
dyspepsy	gipsy	tipsy	dropsy	massy
grassy	glossy	busy	drowsy	

Words ending in *cy*.

legacy	fallacy	supremacy	primacy	legitimacy
intimacy	pharmacy	subordinacy	effeminacy	obstinacy
lunacy	democracy	aristocracy	piracy	accuracy
fleecy	prophecy	secrecy	icy	policy
spicy	juicy	vacancy	dependency	fancy
infancy	brilliancy	luxuriancy	malignancy	repugnancy
occupancy	bankruptcy	fragrancy	vagrancy	expectancy

94 THE NEW RAPID.

hesitancy	instancy	constancy	incumbency	decency
complacency	presidency	ascendency	pedency	tendency
despondency	ardency	agency	exigency	pungency
emergency	deficiency	sufficiency	proficiency	expediency
excellency	indolency	corpulency	vehemency	clemency
inclemency	eminency	pertinency	indifferency	currency
competency	incompetency	potency	impotency	consistency
persistency	existency	insolvency	fluency	frequency
delinquency	idiocy	mercy		

Words ending in *sty*.

yeasty	hasty	dynasty	pasty	modesty
immodesty	majesty	honesty	resty	misty
frosty	thirsty	dusty	gusty	musty
crusty	pastry	ancestry	tapestry	registry
sophestry	ministry	industry		

Words ending in *ity*.

falsity	immensity	propensity	intensity	verbosity
curiosity	animosity	generosity	adversity	diversity
university	perversity	necessity	mendacity	sagacity
pugnacity	capacity	veracity	vivacity	felicity
simplicity	eccentricity	electricity	authenticity	elasticity
velocity	ferocity	atrocity	scarcity	

Words ending in *ely*.

basely	precisely	concisely	wisely	falsely
immensely	intensely	jocosely	closely	loosely
purposely	morosely	coarsely	adversely	diversely
conversely	perversely	transversely	diffusely	profusely
abstrusely	obtusely			

Words ending in *sly*.

heedlessly	needlessly	regardlessly	lifelessly	blamelessly
uselessly	harmlessly	helplessly	fearlessly	thoughtlessly
expressly	grossly	courageously	advantageously	erroneously

PRINCIPLES.

righteously	plenteously	bounteously	sagaciously	graciously
preciously	judiciously	maliciously	deliciously	perniciously
studiously	religiously	harmoniously	piously	variously
seriously	mysteriously	gloriously	meritoriously	notoriously
curiously	furiously	injuriously	luxuriously	licentiously
consciencously	cautiously	obviously	previously	enviously
anxiously	jealously	zealously	marvellously	frivolously
scrupulously	famously	enormously	ravenously	ruinously
poisonously	pompously	dangerously	vigorously	dexterously
vigorously	humorously	monstrously	gratuitously	conspicuously
promiscously	assiduously	mischievously	grievously	strenuously
virtuously				

Words ending in *ly*.

freely	safely	largely	hugely	likely
solely	lamely	namely	tamely	supremely
extremely	timely	comely	homely	handsomely
wholesomely	wearisomely	quarrelsomely	cumbersomely	profanely
humanely	obscenely	serenely	finely	genuinely
lonely	barely	rarely	warely	sincerely
merely	severely	entirely	securely	surely
purely	maturely	requisitely	exquisitely	oppositely
remotely	absolutely	resolutely	bravely	harshly
fourthly	daily	gaily	readily	steadily
needily	speedily	greedily	bodily	helpfully
luckily	lively	family	homily	happily
primarily	summarily	ordinarily	necessarily	voluntarily
verily	merily	weakly	sickly	quickly
neatly	darkly	medically	morally	sensually
actually	punctually	perpetually	loyally	royally
jelly	chilly	silly	folly	holly
wholly	coolly	woolly	firmly	leanly
cleanly	meanly	manly	womanly	humanly
suddenly	greenly	openly	heavenly	ungainly
plainly	certainly	thinly	solemnly	only
commonly	deeply	early	dearly	clearly
nearly	yearly	tenderly	orderly	eagerly

fatherly	motherly	brotherly	southerly	formerly
mannerly	properly	easterly	masterly	westerly
sisterly	fairly	poorly	hourly	

Words ending in *tly*.

ultimately	intimately	proximately	subordinately	obstinately
fortunately	unfortunately	separately	deliberately	moderately
temperately	desperately	stately	privately	adequately
completely	politely	definitely	infinitely	sweetly
quietly	secretly	swiftly	softly	lightly
slightly	nightly	knightly	brightly	sprightly
tightly	unfitly	scantly	abundantly	redundantly
extravagantly	elegantly	arrogantly	gallantly	petulantly
ignorantly	pleasantly	incessantly	instantly	constantly
decently	recently	magnificently	confidently	evidently
providently	ardently	prudently	gently	negligently
diligently	sufficiently	expediently	conveniently	silently
excellently	indolently	violently	insolently	vehemently
permanently	eminently	pertinently	apparently	differently
reverently	currently	presently	competently	penitently
intently	potently	consistently	frequently	subsequently
fervently	faintly	saintly	quaintly	jointly
bluntly	promptly	abruptly	corruptly	smartly
partly	shortly	courtly		

Words ending in *dy* and *ty*.

ready	giddy	muddy	needy	speedy
remedy	comedy	tidy	candy	dandy
handy	sandy	brandy	windy	moody
hardy	wordy	piety	ninety	lofty
eighty	almighty	naughty	laity	city
rapidity	rotundity	commodity	deity	calamity
sublimity	proximity	enmity	deformity	uniformity
conformity	christianity	humanity	sanity	vanity
dignity	malignity	vicinity	trinity	sanguinity
divinity	solemnity	maternity	fraternity	eternity
opportunity	charity	rarity	sincerity	purity
maturity				

Words ending in *dry* and *try*.

laundry	foundry	sundry	entry	sentry
wintry	country	pedentry	pantry	infantry
geometry	poetry	symmetry	idolatry	

Words ending in *ply*, *bly* and *by*.

cheaply	haply	deeply	reply	multiply
imply	simply	comply	apply	supply
probably	applicably	amicably	commendably	peaceably
agreeably	changeably	chargeably	moveably	justifiably
variably	availably	blamably	doubly	pardonably
reasonably	treasonably	seasonably	irreparably	miserably
innumerably	admirably	memorably	durably	measurably
indispensably	profitably	suitably	accoutably	notably
comfortably	immovably	feebly	invincibly	forcibly
audibly	legibly	terribly	horribly	visibly
invisibly	sensibly	possibly	convertibly	humbly
nobly	shabby	baby	flabby	hobby
lobby	stubby	by and by	hereby	thereby
whereby				

Words ending in *fy*.

rarefy	liquefy	pacify	specify	crucify
edify	modify	deify	qualify	disqualify
mollify	nullify	amplify	exemplify	ramify
dignify	indemnify	signify	personify	stupefy
typify	clarify	verify	glorify	terrify
petrify	putrify	purify	falsify	diversify
ratify	gratify	rectify	sanctify	notify
certify	fortify	mortify	testify	justify
beautify	satisfy			

Words ending in *ing*.

facing	piercing	leading	pleading	reading
lading	trading	padding	wadding	bedding
bidding	wedding	pudding	proceeding	preceding

exceeding	bleeding	breeding	biding	riding
building	golding	holding	landing	standing
understanding	misunderst'ding	pending	notwithstanding	binding
winding	sounding	foreboding	according	seeing
all-seeing	lodging	obliging	disobliging	hanging
swinging	longing	catching	watching	fishing
pushing	something	clothing	nothing	plaything
speaking	sneaking	taking	undertaking	painstaking
pricking	rocking	stocking	striking	thinking
husking	dealing	plain-dealing	healing	shambling
peddling	feeling	prevailing	wailing	ceiling
tiling	inkling	twinkling	calling	compelling
swelling	dwelling	shilling	willing	darling
yearling	sterling	scantling	nestling	seeming
trimming	plumbing	becoming	charming	alarming
assuming	gleaning	meaning	gardening	opening
christening	evening	designing	entertaining	lining
repining	winning	cunning	reckoning	reasoning
learning	warning	concerning	discerning	morning
burning	lightning	awning	yawning	going
keeping	chipping	shipping	dripping	tripping
chopping	topping	daring	bearing	hearing
glaring	paring	sparing	wandering	offering
suffering	gathering	entering	muttering	covering
airing	firing	herring	during	coloring
surprising	blessing	dressing	beating	fleeting
meeting	greeting	fighting	waiting	biting
whiting	writing	hand-writing	slanting	relenting
repenting	fainting	painting	bunting	footing
excepting	diverting	lasting	assisting	resisting
befitting	sitting	leaving	shaving	saving
forgiving	thanksgiving	living	thriving	loving
moving	carving	starving	issuing	drawing
flowing	knowing	saying	dying	many things
few things	anything	everything	all things	

Words ending in *ingly*.

enticingly	glancingly	piercingly	exceedingly	understandingly
pretendingly	accordingly	drudgingly	grudgingly	obligingly
revengingly	longingly	snatchingly	scratchingly	touchingly
laughingly	diminishingly	languishingly	sneakingly	mistakingly
mockingly	stealingly	tremblingly	feelingly	triflingly
shufflingly	bunglingly	sparklingly	smilingly	willingly
unwillingly	seemingly	swimmingly	charmingly	threateningly
grinningly	cunningly	discerningly	mourningly	creepingly
limpingly	hopingly	trippingly	sparingly	mutteringly
perseveringly	despairingly	admiringly	alluringly	pleasingly
surprisingly	pressingly	guessingly	doubtingly	slightingly
invitingly	insultingly	enchantingly	resentingly	tauntingly
dartingly	startingly	reportingly	lastingly	everlastingly
boastingly	savingly	livingly	movingly	observingly
flowingly	knowingly	amazingly		

Words ending in *ington*.

Addington	Arrington	Arlington	Barrington	Bennington
Birmington	Blessington	Bloomington	Cardington	Coddington
Covington	Darlington	Eddington	Farmington	Flemmington
Harrington	Huntington	Irvington	Kensington	Lexington
Millington	Paddington	Partington	Readington	Remington
Southington	Torrington	Warrington	Washington	Wellington
Wilmington	Worthington			

SUFFIXES.

There are certain endings which owing to their frequency of occurrence, it is very desirable to contract by a method of syllable abbreviation.

To the right is a full list of the suffixes which are expressed by writing their initial letter in a detached manner across or near the preceding character.

The endings *ment* and *sive* are joined to the initial part of the word without lifting the pen. (See lines 5 and 9).

The suffix *graphically* is expressed by the diminished *g*. (See end of line 3).

Ologically is expressed by adding the *cl* hook to the *l*. (See last part of line 7).

Q is used for both *quish* and *guish*. It is lengthened for *guishment*. (See end of line 8).

SUFFIXES.

ENDINGS.	SIGN.	ILLUSTRATIONS.
1 age	a	
2 ary	ar	
3 graph-y	gr	
4 hood	h	
5 ment	mn	
6 ography	o	
7 ology	l	
8 guish	gq	
9 sive	s	
10 ship	sh	
11 tive	t	
12 tiveness	tns	
13 tory tary	tr	
14 tude	td	
15 uation	u	
16 self	sl	

REVIEW QUESTIONS.

ON THE SUFFIXES.

How is the suffix *age* expressed? What is the difference between the *age* and *ary* signs?

What affix does the *g* sign express.

How write the suffix *graphically?*

Are the signs written across or near the preceding part of a word? *Ans.* Whichever is most convenient.

How is the ending *ment* expressed?

Is it written any different from other signs?

How write *ology?* How write *ologically?*

In what manner is *guishment* expressed?

What different is the *sive* ending from other signs?

What is the difference between the signs for *tive* and *tory?*

How is *tiveness* expressed? How *tively?*

For what two endings does the *tr* stand?

HOW TO WRITE EASILY AND RAPIDLY.

Use a pen, if possible, that is just suited to the hand and that will produce a firm steady line when in quick motion.

Slide the hand easily and naturally across the paper when writing. Do not make a pause after each outline, but observe that the movement is steady and continuous.

Beginners are apt to spend more time in passing from one outline to another than in executing them. This shows how important it is to keep outlines close together. If a pencil is used instead of a pen, accustom yourself to form light lines, otherwise you will find yourself gripping the pencil, which is sure to tire the hand and produce poor outlines. In order to form the habit of writing in an easy running manner, select a familiar sentence containing short words, and write it over and over. Strive to keep the hand in continuous motion and execute the outlines as it passes across the paper. Write the same sentence over again and again, striving to increase the rate of speed at each time of writing. Do not allow the mind to linger with an outline after it is formed but pass quickly to the next.

Practice this from day to day, selecting more difficult matter each time, and practicing it until it can be written without a single pause. This method of speed practice continued for a short time will produce an easy continuous style of writing, and a high rate of speed will be reached almost unconsciously.

THE "*SHUN*" PRINCIPLE.

One of the most common endings in the language is what is known in phonography as *shun*. It may be spelled in English *tion, sion, cion, cian* or *sian* all of which are pronounced *shun*.

This ending is expressed by slightly straightening the *sh* character. (See line 1).

When the *shun* ending follows a circle or loop the line is carried across. (See line 2).

The *shun* stroke can be turned in either direction. (See line 3).

When *s* and *l* follow the *shun* as in *nations* and *national* they are turned on the *shun* stroke. (See lines 4 and 5).

tation and *dation* are expressed by retracing the character preceding the *shun*. (See lines 6 and 7).

shiashun as in *association* is expressed by writing the *shun* stroke upwards. (See line 8).

The *t* is omitted in the ending *ishent*. (See line 9).

In the ending *shul* the *l* takes the place of the *n* in *shun* and hence the *sh* character is diminished in accordance with the diminishing principle to add the *l*. (See line 10).

ish is expressed by the *sh* character which is enlarged in accordance with the enlarging principle for *isht*. (See lines 11 and 12).

It frequently occurs that the prefix *com* and *con* in long words can be omitted, without impairing the legibility. (See line 16).

PRINCIPLES. 105

THE "*SHUN*" PRINCIPLE.

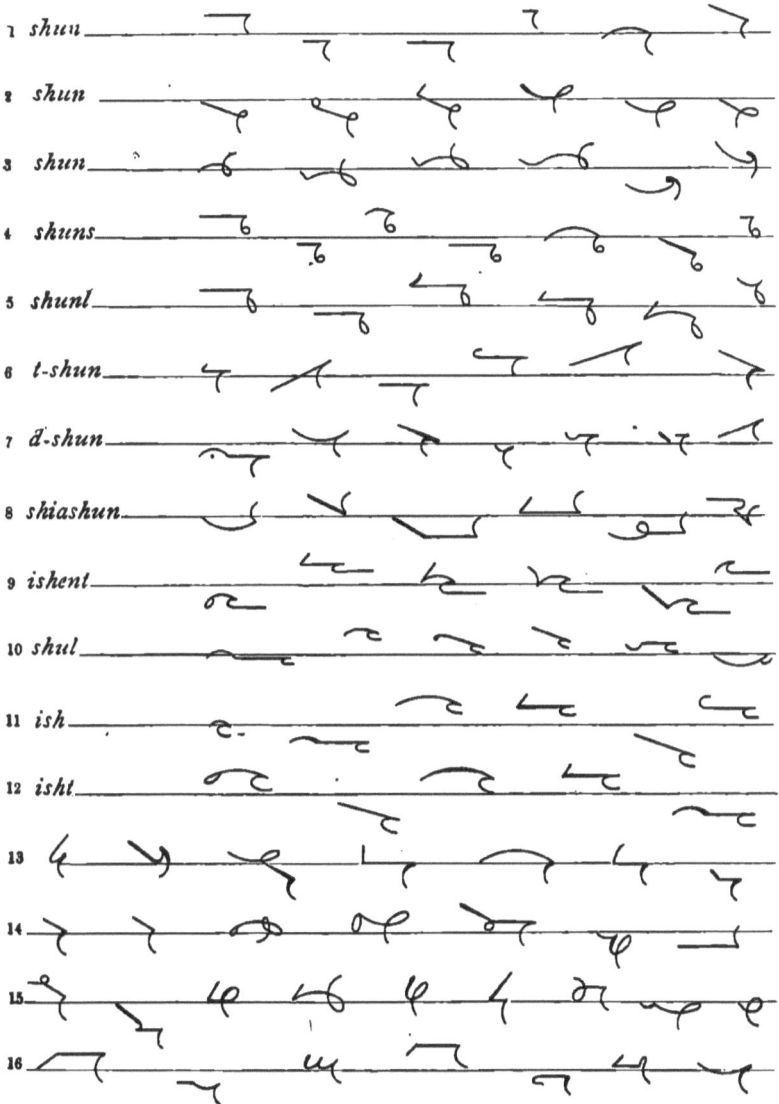

1 shun
2 shun
3 shun
4 shuns
5 shunl
6 t-shun
7 d-shun
8 shiashun
9 ishent
10 shul
11 ish
12 isht
13
14
15
16

REVIEW QUESTIONS.

ON THE *shun* PRINCIPLE

How is the termination *shun* expressed?

How is it written after circles and loops?

Can the *shun* stroke curve in either direction?

How are the endings *tation* and *dation* expressed? Does this retracing bear any relation to previously established principles?

How is the ending *shiashun* expressed?

How is the ending *ishent* written?

What is the difference between the writing of *shunl* and *shul?*

When can the initial syllable *con* and *com* be omitted?

m-nation endings.

abomination	declamation	stagnation	domination
intonation	acclamation	indignation	nomination
carnation	amalgamation	designation	denomination
alternation	proclamation	resignation	incarnation
consternation	exclamation	combination	germination
cremation	termination	fascination	determination
intimation	hallucination	extermination	estimation
ordination	illumination	approximation	subordination
assassination	inflammation	preordination	procrastination
consummation	inordination	destination	affirmation
coordination	predestination	confirmation	imagination
divination	formation	machination	ruination
reformation	declination	damnation	information
inclination	condemnation	transformation	dissemination
donation	nation	crimination	explanation
elimination	coronation	alienation	culmination
personation			

ration endings.

declaration	degeneration	ministration	exhilaration
regeneration	expiration	administration	reparation
veneration	oration	demonstration	preparation
corroboration	prostration	separation	exoneration
decoration	illustration	celebration	remuneration
adoration	duration	vibration	operation
perforation	obduration	desecration	exasperation
invigoration	transfiguration	consecration	desperation
melioration	inauguration	deliberation	vituperation
deterioration	exploration	mensuration	laceration
iteration	commemoration	obliteration	evaporation
corporation	confederation	alteration	incorporation
consideration	adulteration	restoration	moderation
conflagration	narration	exaggeration	migration
aberration	acceleration	emigration	insurrection
toleration	immigration	penetration	conglomeration
admiration	perpetration	enumeration	respiration
arbitration	generation	inspiration	concentration

THE NEW RAPID.

lation endings.

exhalation	contemplation	cumulation	elation
legislation	accumulation	relation	translation
stipulation	revelation	tribulation	population
inflation	ejaculation	depopulation	annihilation
congratulation	assimilation	speculation	ventilation
matriculation	recapitulation	mutilation	articulation
postulation	gesticulation	expostulation	cancellation
inoculation	circulation	appelation	adulation
constellation	modulation	vacillation	regulation
distillation	violation	emulation	immolation
simulation	desolation	dissimnlation	isolation
stimulation	consolation	granulation	

shul endings.

facial	glacial	special	especial
judicial	prejudicial	beneficial	official
artificial	superficial	provincial	social
commercial	crucial	ambrosial	controversial
equinoctial	initial	substantial	circumstantial
credential	providential	prudential	pestilential
differential	reverential	essential	penitential
potential	influential	consequential	nuptial
martial	partial		

shunl endings.

occasional	provisional	processional	professional
progressional	congregational	national	rational
irrational	fractional	traditional	additional
conditional	propositional	intentional	preventional
conventional	notional	devotional	proportional
constitutional			

tation endings.

affectation	plantation	salutation	expectation
lamentation	mutation	dictation	fomentation
permutation	vegetation	alimentation	transmutation
interpretation	fermentation	reputation	habitation

amputation   presentation   computation   citation
representation recitation   ostentation   notation
meditation   rotation   premeditation   agitation
adaptation   imitation   acceptation   limitation
temptation   precipitation   dissertation   palpitation
flirtation   hesitation   importation   transportation
gravitation   exportation   invitation   station
exaltation   devastation   consultation   manifestation
exultation

dativn endings.

gradation   degradation   depredation   elucidation
consolidation   commendation   recommendation   inundation
foundation   accommodation

gation endings.

propagation   legation   delegation   allegation
negation   abnegation   aggregation   congregation
obligation   fumigation   irrigation   litigation
mitigation   investigation   instigation   navigation
circumnavigation   promulgation   elongation   prolongation
abrogation   interrogation   subjugation   conjugation
corrugation

cation endings.

multiplication   implication   complication   application
supplication   explication   duplication   fornication
communication   excommunication   prevarication   fabrication
mastication   intoxication   defalcation   inculcation
suffocation   location   dislocation   vocation
avocation   reavocation   equivocation   invocation
convocation   provocation   altercation   bifurcation
confiscation   education

PREFIXES.

For the purpose of avoiding some very cumbrous outlines, and preserving syllabication, which promotes legibility, signs are employed for the representation of the most difficult and frequently occurring prefixes.

To the left is a full list of the prefixes, which are expressed by writing the sign, *i*, *e*, the first letter, through or near the remaining part of the word.

The prefixes *com-n*, *re*, and *self*, are written without lifting the pen. (See lines 11, 12 and 13).

The prefixes are all written without reference to position, which allows the latter part of a word to be written on position for its vowel.

A light dot is used for the syllables *oc* and *ac*. (See line 15). A heavy dot is employed in the same manner for the syllables *ab* and *ob*.

PREFIXES.

PREFIX.	SIGN.	ILLUSTRATIONS.
1 *accom-n*		
2 *discom-n*		
3 *incom-n*		
4 *miscom-n*		
5 *noncom-n*		
6 *precom-n*		
7 *recom-n*		
8 *self-con*		
9 *uncom-n*		
10 *circum*		
11 *com-n*		
12 *re*		
13 *self*		
14 *trans*		
15 *ac-oc*		
16 *inac*		

REVIEW QUESTIONS.

ON THE PREFIX PRINCIPLE.

What stroke is taken as the sign of a prefix? On what position is it written?

What prefixes are connected with the latter part of a word?

What is the difference between the writing of *re* and *recom?*

How is *ac* and *oc* expressed?

What is the difference between the writing of *inac* and *incom?*

Which is it best to write first, the prefix or the latter part of the word? Why?

Is the prefix written through or detached from the latter part of the word?

www.ingramcontent.com/pod-product-compliance
Lightning Source LLC
Chambersburg PA
CBHW030406170426
43202CB00010B/1505